Challenges for the

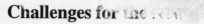

sipri

Stockholm International Peace Research Institute
Frösunda, S-171 53 Solna, Sweden
Cable: SIPRI
Telephone: 46 8/655 97 00
Telefax: 46 8/655 97 33
E-mail: sipri@sipri.se
Internet URL: http://www.sipri.se

Challenges for the New Peacekeepers

SIPRI Research Report No. 12

Edited by

Trevor Findlay

OXFORD UNIVERSITY PRESS
1996

Oxford University Press, Walton Street, Oxford OX2 6DP

Oxford New York

Athens Auckland Bangkok Bombay Calcutta Cape Town Dar es Salaam
Delhi Florence Hong Kong Istanbul Karachi Kuala Lumpur Madras
Madrid Melbourne Mexico City Nairobi Paris Singapore Taipei
Tokyo Toronto

and associated companies in
Berlin Ibadan

Oxford is a trade mark of Oxford University Press

Published in the United States
by Oxford University Press Inc., New York

© SIPRI 1996

British Library Cataloguing in Publication Data
Data available
Library of Congress Cataloguing-in-Publication Data
Findlay, Trevor.
Challenges for the new peacekeepers/ Trevor Findlay
—(SIPRI research report; no. 12) Includes index

ISBN 0–19–829198-1
ISBN 0–19–829199-X (pbk.)

Typeset and originated by Stockholm International Peace Research Institute
Printed in Great Britain on acid-free paper by Biddles Ltd,
Guildford and King's Lynn

Contents

Preface

This volume differs from the increasingly familiar literature on peace-keeping in its emphasis on the challenges faced by individual nations which have, since the end of the cold war, begun to participate in peacekeeping operations for the first time. Without their contributions many of the new, expanded, 'muscular' variety of operations would be impossible. In particular this study focuses on the political and constitutional challenges which some of the most important of these 'new peacekeepers'—Germany, Japan, Russia and the USA—have faced and will continue to face in becoming involved in peace-keeping. Attention is also given to two international organizations—the North Atlantic Treaty Organization (NATO) and the Organization for Security and Co-operation in Europe (OSCE)—which are, respectively, actual and potential new peacekeepers.

One of the findings of this volume is that the effectiveness of peace-keeping activities will be determined not only by the new norms, procedures and institutions but first of all by the determination of states and their government policies—those of both small and medium-sized countries and the great powers.

The chapters in this volume all derive from papers presented at a conference held in Bonn on 21–22 April 1994 on 'Challenges for the New Peacekeepers', jointly organized by the Stockholm International Peace Research Institute (SIPRI) and the Friedrich-Ebert-Stiftung. SIPRI is grateful to the Friedrich-Ebert-Stiftung for funding and helping arrange that event. Dr Erfried Adam, head of the Development Policy Project Group at the Friedrich-Ebert-Stiftung, worked above and beyond the call of duty to organize the meeting. This volume is the second produced by SIPRI's Project on Peacekeeping and Regional Security, which was established in 1993. Its editor is Dr Trevor Findlay, the Leader of this Project, whose work and commitment to producing this book deserve great credit. Special thanks go to the authors of the chapters for their diligence in producing high-quality work to tight deadlines. Olga Hardardóttir and Anneli Berntsson, Research Assistants with the Project, assisted with the research for the volume, and Eve Johansson contributed her considerable editorial skills.

The following analyses of the policies and experiences of the 'new peacekeepers' will, it is hoped, not only be of academic interest but will also make a contribution to the burgeoning international effort to scrutinize the entire peacekeeping enterprise with a view to improving and refining it.

Adam Daniel Rotfeld
Director of SIPRI
October 1995

Acronyms

AHG	Ad Hoc Group on Cooperation in Peacekeeping (NACC)
AIFV	Armoured infantry fighting vehicle
ARF	ASEAN Regional Forum
ARRC	Allied Command Europe Rapid Reaction Corps (NATO)
ASEAN	Association of South-East Asian Nations
AWACS	Airborne warning and control system
BHC	Bosnia–Herzegovina Command (UNPROFOR)
CEE	Central and Eastern Europe
CFE	Conventional Armed Forces in Europe
CIO	Chairman-in-Office (OSCE)
CIS	Commonwealth of Independent States
CJTF	Combined Joint Task Force
CPC	Conflict Prevention Centre (OSCE)
CSBM	Confidence- and security-building measure
CSCE	Conference on Security and Co-operation in Europe
DMZ	Demilitarized zone
EC	European Community
ECOMOG	ECOWAS Monitoring Group (in Liberia)
ECOWAS	Economic Organization of West African States
ECR	Electronic combat and reconnaissance aircraft
EU	European Union
FMLN	Frente Farabundo Martí para la Liberación Nacional (Farabundo Marti National Liberation Front, El Salvador)
FRG	Federal Republic of Germany
FSC	Forum for Security Co-operation (OSCE)
GDR	German Democratic Republic
HCNM	High Commissioner on National Minorities (OSCE)
HLPG	High Level Planning Group (OSCE)
MD	Military District (Russia)
MFO	Multinational Force and Observers (in Sinai)
MICIVIH	Mission Civile Internationale en Haiti (International Civilian Mission to Haiti)
MINURSO	UN Mission for the Referendum in Western Sahara

MIOB	Mission Internationale d'Observation au Burundi (International Observation Mission in Burundi)
MND	Multinational division
MNF	Multinational Force in Haiti
MOD	Ministry of Defence (Russia)
MRD	Motorized Rifle Division (Russia)
NAC	North Atlantic Council
NACC	North Atlantic Cooperation Council
OAS	Organization of American States
OAU	Organization of African Unity
ODIHR	Office for Democratic Institutions and Human Rights (OSCE)
ONUC	Organisation des Nations Unies au Congo (UN Organization in the Congo)
ONUCA	Observadores de las Naciones Unidas en Centroamérica (UN Observer Mission in Central America)
ONUMOZ	UN Operation in Mozambique
ONUSAL	Misión de las Nacionas Unidas en El Salvador (UN Observer Mission in El Salvador)
ONUVEH	UN Mission to Verify the Election in Haiti
ONUVEN	Observadores de las Naciones Unidas para la Verificación de las Elecciones en Nicaragua (UN Verification Mission for the Nicaraguan Elections)
OSCE	Organization for Security and Co-operation in Europe
PDD	Presidential Decision Directive (USA)
PFP	Partnership for Peace
RENAMO	Résistência Nacional Moçambicana (Mozambican National Resistance)
ROE	Rules of engagement
RRF	Rapid Reaction Force (in Bosnia and Herzegovina)
SAM	Sanctions Assistance Mission (OSCE)
SDF	Self-Defense Forces (Japan)
SHAPE	Supreme Headquarters Allied Powers Europe (NATO)
SOP	Standing operating procedures
SPPKF	South Pacific Peacekeeping Force
UAR	United Arab Republic
UNAMIC	UN Advance Mission in Cambodia
UNAMIR	UN Assistance Mission for Rwanda
UNAVEM	UN Angola Verification Mission

UNCRO	UN Confidence Restoration Operation in Croatia
UNDOF	UN Disengagement Observer Force (in Syria)
UNDP	United Nations Development Programme
UNEF	UN Emergency Force (in Israel and Egypt)
UNFICYP	UN Peacekeeping Force in Cyprus
UNGOMAP	UN Good Office Mission in Afghanistan and Pakistan
UNHCR	UN High Commissioner for Refugees
UNIFIL	UN Interim Force in Lebanon
UNIKOM	UN Iraq–Kuwait Observation Mission
UNIPOM	UN India–Pakistan Observation Mission
UNITAF	Unified Task Force (in Somalia)
UNITAR	UN Institute for Training and Research
UNMIH	UN Mission in Haiti
UNMOGIP	UN Military Observer Group in India and Pakistan
UNOGIL	UN Observer Group in Lebanon
UNOMIG	UN Observer Mission in Georgia
UNOMIL	UN Observer Mission in Liberia
UNOMSA	UN Observer Mission in South Africa
UNOMUR	UN Observer Mission Uganda–Rwanda
UNOSOM	UN Operation in Somalia
UNPF	UN Peace Forces (incorporates after March 1995 UNPROFOR, UNCRO and UNPREDEP)
UNPREDEP	UN Preventive Deployment Force (in Macedonia)
UNPROFOR	UN Protection Force (in the former Yugoslavia 1992–March 1995; from March 1995 in Bosnia and Herzegovina)
UNSCOM	UN Special Commission on Iraq
UNSF	UN Security Force (in Irian Jaya)
UNTSO	UN Truce Supervision Organization
UNTAC	UN Transitional Authority in Cambodia
UNTAG	UN Transition Assistance Group (in Namibia)
UNTEA	UN Transitional Executive Authority (in Irian Jaya)
UNTSO	UN Truce Supervision Organization (in Egypt/Israel/ Lebanon/Syria)
UNV	UN Volunteers
UNYOM	UN Yemen Observation Mission
URNG	Unidad Revolucionaria Nacional Guatemalteca (Guatemalan National Revolutionary Unity)
WEU	Western European Union

1. The new peacekeepers and the new peacekeeping

Trevor Findlay

I. Introduction

Peacekeeping is a child of the cold war, born of the United Nations' frustration at its inability to enforce the peace as envisaged in its Charter and its desire to do more to affect the course of international armed conflict than simply mediating and conciliating from a distance. Neither mentioned by name nor given a specific legal basis in the UN Charter, peacekeeping evolved pragmatically in response to the limited room for manœuvre afforded the UN by the East–West conflict. Peacekeeping is 'in many respects a reversal of the use of military personnel foreseen in the Charter . . . Its practitioners have no enemies, are not there to win and can use force only in self-defence. Its effectiveness depends on voluntary cooperation'.[1] In 1988 the UN peacekeeping forces were awarded the Nobel Peace Prize. With a long list of successes to its credit, peacekeeping is arguably the UN's finest invention.

As a product of its time, however, peacekeeping was bound to change once the cold war ended. Since 1989 it has cast off its cold war shackles and vastly extended both the range and the pace of its activities. No longer confined to quietly monitoring borders, as in Kashmir since 1949, or conducting somewhat more delicate conflict management tasks, as in Lebanon since 1978, UN peacekeepers are now engaged in complex nation-building exercises that have stretched the limits of both the theory and practice of peacekeeping. As a New Zealand peacekeeper has put it, 'the days of turning up equipped with only good intentions, blue berets and a cut lunch are over'.[2]

The end of the cold war has also introduced scores of new players to peacekeeping. For many of these 'new peacekeepers' there are great challenges in participating for the first time, not just because

---

[1] WEU document 1366, 1993, cited in Roos, J. G., 'The perils of peacekeeping', *Armed Forces Journal International*, Dec. 1993, p. 13.

[2] 'New Zealand in the Security Council 1993–94', New Zealand Ministry of Foreign Affairs and Trade, *Information Bulletin*, no. 52 (Mar. 1995), p. 31.

they are new to peacekeeping but because of the dramatic changes that peacekeeping has undergone.

This chapter aims first to determine who the new peacekeepers are. Second, it analyses the nature of the 'new peacekeeping' that has emerged since 1989. Third, it examines the challenges that the new peacekeeping poses to the new peacekeepers and how they have affected their participation and performance.

II. The new peacekeepers

UN peacekeeping traditionally relied on a handful of states to provide the bulk of the personnel required. These were mostly medium-sized developed states, principally Australia, Austria, Canada, Denmark, Finland, Ireland, New Zealand, Norway and Sweden, and larger developing states like India and Pakistan. A handful of smaller developing states, particularly Fiji, Ghana, Nepal and Senegal, were also prominent. However, beginning with the deployment of UNTAG[3] in Namibia between April 1989 and March 1990, a period during which the cold war is widely considered to have ended, there has been an enormous increase in the number of states involved in UN peacekeeping. In 1988, before UNTAG, only 26 countries were involved. By November 1994 there were 76.[4]

The main reason for the increasing involvement has been increased need. With the end of the cold war more of the world's armed conflicts became ripe for negotiated settlements as client states lost their superpower mentors and the Security Council achieved a new unity in actively seeking such settlements. The end of the cold war also unleashed new conflicts in the Balkan states and several of the former Soviet republics. The conflict resolution tool of choice in almost all cases has been peacekeeping or some variant thereof: more peacekeeping operations have been established since 1989 than in the previous 45 years of the UN's history. While in 1988 the UN operated just 5 peacekeeping missions, by its peak year of 1993 it had 18.[5]

---

[3] The full titles of UN and other peacekeeping operations are not spelled out in each chapter. The reader is referred to the list of acronyms at the front of the book.

[4] UN Press Release, SG/SM/95/52, 3 Mar. 1995, p. 2; and UN, *United Nations Peace-keeping Information Notes*, DPI713067Rev. 4, United Nations, Feb. 1995, pp. 239–42.

[5] UN, Supplement to An Agenda for Peace: Position Paper of the Secretary-General on the Occasion of the Fiftieth Anniversary of the United Nations, UN document A/50/60, S/1995/1, 3 Jan. 1995; and UN, *United Nations Peace-keeping Operations*, Background Note (United Nations Information Centre for the Nordic Countries: Copenhagen, Oct. 1993).

Other international organizations have also increasingly launched peacekeeping operations. Depending on how one classifies them, the number of non-UN peacekeeping missions has increased from one in 1988 (the MFO in Sinai) to at least six. More peacekeeping personnel have been deployed abroad than at any time in history. In 1988 the UN had only 9950 troops in the field; by 1993 it had a record 80 000.[6] At the end of July 1995, approximately 65 000 military personnel were deployed in 16 UN peacekeeping operations.[7] The numbers of civilian police and other civilian personnel have also increased substantially. As of the end of July 1995 the UN had 1700 civilian police in the field (an increase from 35 in 1988) and 6000 civilian personnel (from 1500 in 1988).

Who are the new peacekeepers?

For the purposes of this volume the new peacekeepers are broadly defined as those states which since 1989 have participated in a UN peacekeeping mission for the first time in their history. Forty-nine states fall into this category (see table 1.1). Hence more than half of the current approximately 80 UN peacekeeping contributors are 'new'. All new contributors of troops, military observers or civilian police are listed, whatever the size or character of their contribution. Countries which have only contributed civilian personnel other than police are not included. Although some of the challenges facing civilian personnel in peacekeeping missions are considered, in this volume the emphasis is on military involvement. A peacekeeping mission has been taken to be one listed by the UN as such[8] and mandated implicitly or explicitly under Chapter VI of the UN Charter relating to the peaceful settlement of disputes, although they may also contain some elements of peace enforcement as in the cases of UNPROFOR and UNOSOM II.[9]

---

[6] Supplement to An Agenda for Peace (note 5); and *United Nations Peace-keeping Operations* (note 5).

[7] UN, Report of the Secretary-General on the work of the Organization, UN document A/50/1, 22 Aug. 1995, p. 81; and Supplement to An Agenda for Peace (note 5).

[8] See the *United Nations Peacekeeping Information Notes* series published by the Department of Peace-keeping Operations in New York.

[9] This volume does not consider 'pure' peace enforcement missions authorizable by the Security Council under Chapter VII of the UN Charter relating to peace enforcement which are clearly not peacekeeping. Such missions may be conducted by forces under the UN flag, as in Korea in the early 1950s, or by a non-UN multilateral force or single state authorized to act by the Security Council, as in the case of Operation Desert Storm against Iraq in 1991.

Table 1.1. First-time participants in UN peacekeeping and observer missions since 1989[1]

Country	First mission	Year
Albania	UNOMIG	1994
Algeria	UNAMIC	1991
Barbados	UNTAG	1989
Botswana	ONUMOZ	1993
Brunei Darussalam	UNTAC	1992
Bulgaria	UNTAC	1992
Cameroon	UNTAC	1992
Cape Verde	ONUMOZ	1993
Chad	UNAMIR	1994
China	UNTAG	1989
Congo	UNAVEM I	1989
Costa Rica	UNTAG	1989
Cuba	UNOMIG	1994
Czechoslovakia[2]	UNAVEM I	1989
Czech Republic[2]	UNPROFOR	1993
Djibouti	UNMIH	1994
Egypt[3]	UNTAG	1989
El Salvador	MINURSO	1995
Estonia	UNPROFOR	1995
Germany[4]	UNAMIC	1991
FRG[4]	UNTAG	1989
GDR[4]	UNTAG	1989
Greece	UNTAG	1989
Guatemala	UNMIH	1994
Guinea Bissau	UNAVEM II	1991
Guyana	UNTAG	1989
Honduras	MINURSO	1991
Jamaica	UNTAG	1989
Japan	UNTAC	1992
Jordan	UNAVEM I	1989
Korea, South	UNOSOM II	1993
Kuwait	UNOSOM II	1993
Lithuania	UNPROFOR	1994
Luxembourg	UNPROFOR	1992
Malawi	UNAMIR	1993
Mali[5]	UNAMIR	1993
Namibia	UNTAC	1992
Niger	UNAMIR	1994
Romania	UNIKOM	1991
Russian Federation	UNIKOM	1991

Country	First mission	Year
Saudi Arabia	UNOSOM II	1993
Singapore	UNTAG	1989
Slovakia[2]	UNPROFOR	1993
Spain	UNAVEM I	1989
Switzerland	UNTAG	1989
Togo	UNTAG	1989
Trinidad and Tobago	UNTAG	1989
Uganda	UNOSOM II	1993
Ukraine	UNPROFOR	1992
United Arab Emirates	UNOSOM I	1993
USA[6]	UNIKOM	1991
Zimbabwe	UNAVEM II	1991

[1] Only missions listed by the UN as peacekeeping missions are included.

[2] On 31 Dec. 1992 Czechoslovakia split into the Czech Republic and Slovakia.

[3] Participated in ONUC 1960–61 as the United Arab Republic.

[4] The Federal Republic of Germany and the German Democratic Republic merged into one state in 1990.

[5] Participated in ONUC in 1960 as a part of the Federation of Mali (now Mali and Senegal). Senegal participated for the first time as an independent state in UNEF II in 1974.

[6] The USA was involved in 2 earlier missions, UNTSO (1948 to date) and UNMOGIP (1949–54).

An additional 21 states are listed in table 1.2. These are states which have never been involved in a UN mission, even during the post-cold war years, but which have contributed for the first time to a non-UN peacekeeping mission since 1989. Missions established by Russia, in cooperation with the Commonwealth of Independent States (CIS) or trilaterally with other former Soviet republics, have been taken into account, although their 'peacekeeping' character is doubtful because of their unconventional operating procedures, especially their willingness to use force, the predominance of Russian forces and the extent of Russian involvement in the conflicts themselves.[10] They are of interest here primarily because of the involvement of several new former Soviet republics among the peacekeepers and their exposure to at least some of the norms and procedures of traditional peacekeeping.

[10] Russian political parlance does not differentiate between peacekeeping, peacemaking and peace enforcement. The term used in Russia (*mirotvorchestvo*), directly translated, means 'peace creation'; this could cover a very broad range of activities, from political mediation to combat operations aimed at 'imposing peace'.

Table 1.2. First-time participants in non-UN peacekeeping and observer missions since 1989[1]

Country	First mission	Year
Antigua and Barbuda	MNF	1994
Armenia	OSCE Skopje[2]	1992
Bahamas	MNF	1994
Belize	MNF	1994
Benin	MNF	1994
Dominica	MNF	1994
Gambia	ECOMOG	1990
Georgia	South Ossetia[3]	1992
Grenada	MNF	1994
Israel	MNF	1994
Kazakhstan	CIS Tajikistan[4]	1993
Kyrgyzstan	CIS Tajikistan	1993
Mauritania	Opération Turquoise	1994
Moldova	Moldova Joint Force[5]	1992
St Kitts and Nevis	MNF	1994
St Lucia	MNF	1994
St Vincent and Grenadines	MNF	1994
Tanzania	ECOMOG	1994
Tonga	SPPKF	1994
Uzbekistan	CIS Tajikistan	1993
Vanuatu	SPPKF	1994

[1] Only countries which have never participated in UN missions. In addition to states, 3 non-state actors (South Ossetia and North Ossetia in Georgia and the Trans-Dniester region in Moldova) are involved in Russian-led peacekeeping operations in former Soviet republics.

[2] OSCE Spillover Mission to the Former Yugoslav Republic of Macedonia.

[3] South Ossetia Joint Force in Georgia.

[4] CIS Tajikistan Buffer Force in Tajikistan (Afghan border).

[5] Moldova Joint Force in Moldova (Trans-Dniester).

There are some complications in determining exactly who is a new peacekeeper. Some states which are listed here as 'new' participated previously as different entities: Egypt contributed to ONUC as one half of the United Arab Republic (UAR), along with Syria; Russia is included as a new nation although the Soviet Union participated in a limited number of peacekeeping missions in the Middle East with a tiny number of observers;[11] the new nations that emerged from the

[11] In addition to helping airlift food at the beginning of the Congo operation.

former Soviet Union are considered to be new peacekeepers, as are the unified Germany (although the two former German states had brief experience in UNTAG), the Czech Republic and Slovakia (even though Czechoslovakia participated as a unified state in UNAVEM I in Angola).

Finally, the USA is also considered a new peacekeeper for the purposes of this volume—despite the fact that it assisted with some UN peacekeeping missions during the cold war[12]—because its pre-1989 role was relatively minor, it did not provide ground troops and, most importantly, because it has played such a crucial role in the subsequent new peacekeeping.

Motivations for participation

The motivations of the new peacekeepers probably differ little from those of the old, although a higher proportion of newcomers may be participating because of outside pressure, either from their allies or from the UN Secretary-General or Secretariat or some other international organization. For instance, many of the Caribbean states (and Israel) which participated in the MNF in Haiti and thereafter in UNMIH, were pressured to participate by the USA in order to lend a multilateral character to a US-dominated mission. A similar process occurred in assembling the forces for UNITAF. Russia pressured fellow CIS members to join it in peacekeeping in Tajikistan.

Still, many states volunteer willingly. Although much is made of so-called peacekeeping fatigue, so keen have states been to participate in some of the 'safer' missions that a number of such missions have been 'over-subscribed'. More states were willing to volunteer troops for UNAVEM II and UNMIH, for instance, than could be accommodated.[13]

Motives are invariably mixed. Altruism is one factor. Some of the 'old' peacekeepers like Canada, Norway and Sweden have regarded participation in peacekeeping as the quintessence of good inter-

[12] The USA has contributed aircraft, military observers, pilots, radio operators and mediators to UNTSO and provided military observers and aircraft to UNMOGIP in its early years. US experience with other UN operations during the cold war was restricted to providing airlift and technical support. US experience with non-UN peacekeeping included the highly successful and in some respects unprecedented mission in Sinai, the MFO.

[13] Statement by Dr Emilio Cardenas, Argentine Ambassador to the United Nations, 25th Vienna Seminar, International Peace Academy, Vienna, 4 Mar. 1995.

national citizenship. This may indeed have been a primary motivation in the days when peacekeeping was a relatively unpublicized back-water of international activity, but altruism is today more likely to be outweighed by other factors. Peacekeeping has acquired a certain cachet and participation is seen as enhancing national prestige and independence. Such factors appear especially important to the newly independent states of the former Soviet Union and former Warsaw Pact members whose foreign policies were essentially subordinated to that of the Soviet state for 40 years. Public opinion may, of course, still steel the altruism of governments and cause them to act, par-ticularly in humanitarian crises, as in the case of Somalia.

For states which expect to be favoured candidates for permanent membership of the Security Council (if and when it is expanded), par-ticipation in peacekeeping has become a *sine qua non*. All the most widely touted candidates—Brazil, Germany, India, Indonesia, Japan, Nigeria and Pakistan—are now important contributors. Others hope their participation will increase their influence on the course of inter-national events generally and more specifically in the areas in which peacekeeping operations are deployed. New Zealand's contribution to UNPROFOR during its term as a non-permanent member of the Security Council was at least partly inspired by a desire to enhance its credibility and influence in Council debates on the situation in the former Yugoslavia.

Some new peacekeepers, like Spain, see peacekeeping as contribut-ing, inchoately, to their national security.[14] Others see a more direct link. The members of the Association of South-East Asian Nations (ASEAN),[15] all of which participated in UNTAC in Cambodia, saw that operation as being decidedly in their national security interests.

Some new peacekeepers may even view participation in peacekeep-ing as a down payment for the day when they themselves will need the assistance of the international community. This may be one of the principal motivations of the three Baltic states, Estonia, Latvia and Lithuania, which live in the shadow of Russia. The Baltic states also undoubtedly see participation in peacekeeping as demonstrating their ability to contribute to the purposes of the NATO alliance in which

---

[14] Ordóñez, F. F., 'Introduccion', *Misiones de Paz Militares Españoles en el mundo 1979–1991* [Spanish peace missions throughout the world 1979–1991], (Ministerio de Defensa: Madrid, 1991), p. 9.

[15] ASEAN was formed in 1968 by Indonesia, Malaysia, the Philippines, Singapore and Thailand. Brunei Darussalam joined in 1984 and Viet Nam in 1995.

they ardently hope for membership. For others, such as Egypt, El Salvador, Greece, Israel, Jordan, Namibia, South Korea and Zimbabwe, participation in peacekeeping is a way of repaying a debt for the peacekeeping operations of which they have been beneficiaries in the past.

States in which the military is not entirely under civilian control, such as Argentina, may view peacekeeping as a means both of keeping their armed forces occupied outside the country rather than meddling in domestic affairs and of helping to rehabilitate them after an authoritarian era in which their integrity and professionalism were compromised. As Argentina's Defence Minister, Oscar Camilión, has diplomatically expressed it, Argentina's participation in peacekeeping 'not only gives members of the armed forces a deep feeling of professional pride, but also an international outlook which is very much helping to consolidate the military as a pillar of the constitutional system'.[16]

A less edifying motivation for some of the new peacekeepers from the developing world may be a desire to profit from the reimbursements for the costs of troop contributions (over and above those they would have incurred if their forces had remained home). This is not confined to the new peacekeepers: Fiji's involvement in peacekeeping since 1978 has reportedly been a 'significant source of foreign exchange'.[17] Some poorer states can indeed make a profit on such transactions, but the UN is usually so slow in paying and the amount so relatively niggardly that this cannot be a sole motivating factor. Even Fiji has threatened to quit peacekeeping unless it is 'reimbursed' more promptly.

The armed forces of some countries may also benefit by receiving equipment from better-equipped force contributors during peacekeeping operations, as happened in UNOSOM II in Somalia. In Bosnia and Herzegovina, Germany is supplying protective vehicles to the Pakistani contingent, while the Jordanians are receiving US assistance.[18]

Perhaps most important to all contributing militaries, whether from rich or poor countries, is the invaluable overseas experience that peacekeeping operations provide them in peacetime and the training

[16] Camilión, O., 'Argentina', *Defence and Security Review 1995*, p. 15.

[17] Scobell, A., 'Politics, professionalism and peacekeeping: an analysis of the 1987 military coup in Fiji', *Comparative Politics*, vol. 26, no. 2 (Jan. 1994), p. 190.

[18] *International Defense Review*, vol. 27, no. 11 (1994), p. 10.

and contacts with other military forces that may ensue. Some military establishments may not, however, favour excessive involvement in peacekeeping, either in general or in relation to particular missions. Many will take the view of the Australian military, which is that peacekeeping is a useful exercise, affording operational and training benefits, but that if over-emphasized it risks detracting from the nation's own defence needs.[19]

In some cases it will not be the military (or only the military) that seeks a national role in peacekeeping but the foreign ministry, perhaps prodded by its mission to the UN in New York, in turn perhaps pressured by a UN Secretary-General and Secretariat desperately seeking contributors. The Secretary-General's attempts since 1993 to ensure the credibility of the new UN Standby Forces Arrangement by sending a military delegation to as many member states as possible to plead for and organize pledges of contributions may also have increased the number of actual participants in peacekeeping.

Categories of new peacekeepers

Several categories of new peacekeepers are discernible. The first, perhaps surprisingly, comprises three of the five permanent members of the Security Council—China, Russia and the USA. All the five permanent members of the Security Council had largely forgone involvement during the cold war because of the danger that their rivalries would be injected into the very conflicts from which peacekeeping was designed to isolate them. France and the UK were partial exceptions.[20] In contrast, China completely abjured participation in peacekeeping during the cold war, involving itself for the first time in 1989 in UNTAG. Since the end of the cold war both Russia and the USA have participated in several UN missions. Russia has even provided ground troops, as in UNPROFOR, and organized and taken the preponderant role in peacekeeping operations on its troubled periphery.

---

[19] Cheeseman, G., 'Defence and the UN: the two-edged sword', *Unity* (Canberra), June 1995, p. 8.

[20] France participated in UNIFIL in Lebanon, the UK in UNFICYP in Cyprus. Both also participated extensively in non-UN missions and gained experience relevant to peacekeeping in numerous situations during the decline of their respective colonial empires. Britain's experience in Malaya, Zimbabwe and Northern Ireland foreshadowed much of today's complex multi-purpose UN missions. France's role in francophone Africa since decolonization has been intermittently that of peacekeeper between warring factions competing to control its former colonies.

The USA has dominated major non-UN (but UN-authorized) missions—UNITAF in Somalia and the MNF in Haiti. By 1995 it was also participating in a range of regular UN peacekeeping operations, including UNTSO, UNIKOM, MINURSO, UNPROFOR (in Croatia and Macedonia), UNMIH and UNOMIG.[21] Its preference continues to be to provide support services rather than ground troops.

A second group of new peacekeepers comprises countries that were previously unacceptable because of their association with one of the cold war blocs or because of other political sensitivities: these include Bulgaria, Cuba, Israel, Romania, South Korea and Spain.[22] A third group comprises the defeated World War II allies, called the 'enemy states' in the UN Charter.[23] Germany and Japan, moving finally to assume all the rights and responsibilities of international citizenship, have begun incrementally to participate in peacekeeping. (Italy has participated in peacekeeping operations for some time, mostly by providing observers or air transport.[24]) A fourth category of new peacekeepers includes newly independent states such as Estonia, Kyrgyzstan, Lithuania, Namibia and Ukraine, which never had the opportunity to participate before. A final group includes a wide variety of states which are participating for the first time simply because the current need for peacekeeping forces is so great. These include Brunei, Cape Verde, Costa Rica, Guyana, Luxembourg, Saudi Arabia, Singapore, Switzerland and Uganda. While their contributions may seem inconsequential compared to those of larger states, they broaden the support base for UN peacekeeping and the range of experience and capabilities available for future missions.

International organizations besides the UN are also becoming involved as new peacekeepers, as sponsors and organizers of peacekeeping missions, or at the very least as developers of peacekeeping doctrine for missions to be employed in the future: these include the European Union (EU), the Organization for Security and Co-operation in Europe (OSCE), NATO, the North Atlantic Cooperation Council (NACC) and the CIS.[25]

---

[21] Holt, V. K. *Briefing Book on Peacekeeping: The US Role in United Nations Peace Operations*, 2nd edn (Council for a Livable World Education Fund: Washington, DC, 1995), p. 12.

[22] *United Nations Peacekeeping Information Notes*, DPI713067Rev. 4 (note 4), p. 241.

[23] Charter of the United Nations, Article 53.2.

[24] Including UNEF I, UNTSO, UNOGIL, UNYOM, UNIPOM, ONUC, UNFICYP and UNIFIL.

[25] See also chapters 4, 7 and 8 in this volume.

III. The new peacekeeping

In its broadest sense peacekeeping is the deployment of UN or other multilateral personnel in the field as a tool of conflict prevention, management or resolution. Attempts at defining peacekeeping more specifically have always been bedevilled by the peculiar nature of the beast. Peacekeeping is not mentioned in the UN Charter, it has never been guided by established theory or doctrine, the term was invented long after praxis had begun and improvisation has characterized its evolution ever since.

The UN has traditionally defined a peacekeeping operation as one 'involving military personnel, but without enforcement powers, undertaken by the United Nations to help maintain or restore international peace and security in areas of conflict'.[26] Despite the somewhat heady language of the latter part of this definition the early generation of peacekeeping operations were mostly little more than ad hoc holding operations designed to freeze in place erstwhile combatants and their lines of control until a peaceful solution to a conflict presented itself. Prime examples are the border-monitoring operations in Kashmir (UNMOGIP) and the Middle East (UNTSO). The three traditional key characteristics of such missions were: (*a*) the consent of all the parties to the presence and activities of the mission; (*b*) the impartiality of the peacekeepers in their relationship with the parties; and (*c*) minimum use of force, only as a last resort and only in self-defence or to defend the carrying out of the mission. Such missions have mostly been established explicitly or implicitly under Chapter VI of the UN Charter relating to the peaceful settlement of disputes.

After 1989 there evolved quite rapidly, although haphazardly and piecemeal, what has been widely recognized as a new form of peacekeeping, variously called second-generation, muscular, extended, wider, advanced, broader, protected, aggravated or enforced.[27] This new peacekeeping has been characterized by a comprehensive, even holistic, proactive approach to seeking peaceful settlements and an increasing willingness on the part of the UN to breach rigid interpretations of the right of states to non-interference in their internal

[26] UN, *The Blue Helmets: A Review of United Nations Peace-keeping*, 2nd edn (United Nations: New York, 1990), p. 4.

[27] For arguments that dispute the novelty of the new peacekeeping, see James, A., 'Is there a second generation of peacekeeping?', *International Peacekeeping*, vol. 1, no. 4 (Sep./Nov. 1994), pp. 110–13.

affairs. The holding operation of yesteryear has been superseded by the multifunctional operation linked to and integrated with an entire peace process. Where peacekeepers once studiously avoided tackling the root causes of armed conflict in favour of containment and de-escalation, they are now mandated to seek just and lasting solutions.

Moreover, peacekeepers today are most likely to be confronted by intra-state wars, a type of conflict in which the UN has traditionally not become involved (with the significant exceptions of the Congo, Cyprus and Lebanon). Of the 5 peacekeeping operations deployed in early 1988, only 1 was in a situation of intra-state conflict.[28] Of the 21 operations established since then only 8 have related to interstate wars, whereas 13 have related to intra-state conflicts. (Some of the latter, notably in the former Yugoslavia, also have interstate dimensions.) Of the 11 operations established since January 1992, all but 2 relate to intra-state wars.

Many of these new operations have been characterized by the erosion or even the absence of consent of the parties to the presence and activities of UN forces. Since the end of the cold war the Security Council has been willing to override a strict interpretation of the consent rule because of the political or strategic importance of a particular conflict, the scale of the threat it poses to international security, a calculation that the conflict is ripe for settlement despite the absence of appropriate levels of consent, or the need to be seen to be acting in a crisis. In some cases the new peacekeeping has been accompanied by a greater propensity to use force.

Some peacekeeping missions have even had peace enforcement elements authorized under Chapter VII of the UN Charter grafted onto them, as in the case of UNOSOM II and UNPROFOR. On occasions a non-UN multinational force has been authorized by the Security Council essentially to conduct a peacekeeping operation, but under a Chapter VII mandate, as in the case of Opération Turquoise by France in Rwanda and the MNF in Haiti.

The newness of the new peacekeeping should not be exaggerated. At least three missions before the end of the cold war—ONUC in the Congo, UNSF/UNTEA in Irian Jaya and UNIFIL in Lebanon—presaged the type of missions that would come after it.

---

[28] Supplement to An Agenda for Peace (note 5) p. 3.

IV. Challenges for the new peacekeepers

The consequences of involvement in the new peacekeeping for states participating for the first time are immense. Political and constitutional complexities may delay, constrain or rule out their participation; the military or other personnel being offered may not be trained or equipped for peacekeeping; governments may not wish to accept UN command and control of their forces; public opinion may not countenance casualties or tolerate the subtleties, ambiguities and frustrations of peacekeeping; and, for a variety of reasons, the new peacekeepers on the ground may not shape up.

Lacking the experience and training of the 'old' peacekeepers, the newcomers have been thrown into the peacekeeping enterprise just as its boundaries have been widened, its content vastly expanded and some of its previous norms and assumptions called into question. In a sense all participants in the new peacekeeping are new peacekeepers since they are encountering a largely unfamiliar type of undertaking. The new peacekeepers have had to learn all the lessons of peacekeeping immediately. Since the traditional ethos of peacekeeping arguably remains the bedrock on which the new peacekeeping also operates this gives the old peacekeepers a decided advantage. This was most evident in Somalia, where unfamiliarity with or scepticism about the traditional approach to peacekeeping, particularly among US personnel, was one of the factors which drew UNOSOM II into peace enforcement operations for which it was not prepared.[29] The report of the UN Commission of Enquiry into the débâcle in Mogadishu in 1993 recommended, as a consequence, that all future UN missions include experienced peacekeepers.[30]

The new peacekeepers are, at least in theory, expected to carry out the same tasks as the more experienced. However, particular UN force commanders may assign new peacekeepers less demanding tasks, either at the request of their government, because of operational considerations or because it is known that the troops are unable to carry

[29] For details, see Claesson, P. and Findlay, T., 'Case studies on peacekeeping: UNOSOM II, UNTAC and UNPROFOR', *SIPRI Yearbook 1994* (Oxford University Press: Oxford, 1994), appendix 1B, pp. 62–66.

[30] UN, Report of the Commission of Inquiry established pursuant to Security Council Resolution 885 (1993) to investigate armed attacks on UNOSOM II personnel which led to casualties among them, New York, 24 Feb. 1994, appended to UN, Note by the Secretary-General, UN document S/1994/653, 1 June 1994, p. 48.

out more arduous assignments. The Japanese Self-Defense Forces (SDF) contingent in UNTAC, for instance, was not assigned to dangerous areas because of constitutional restrictions on its use of force in self-defence. This is not to imply that all the new peacekeepers are less capable as military forces than the old. Even the well-equipped and trained military of a highly developed country like Japan can flounder when confronted with the intricacies and subtleties of the new peacekeeping. In Cambodia Japanese troops reportedly experienced 'initial confusion and a lengthy shakedown period'.[31]

Some of the specific difficulties that the new peacekeepers have encountered will be considered in the following sections.

The decision to participate

For many of the new peacekeepers the decision to participate in the first place can be far from uncomplicated and may involve the most sensitive and contested of political and constitutional issues, as in the German and Japanese cases. Even after extensive national debates, the problems will recur, especially if peacekeeping missions encounter fragile or deteriorating consent of the parties and 'mission creep' into peace enforcement results. Even old peacekeepers encounter such problems. The legislation under which Finnish peacekeepers are dispatched is ill adapted to the new peacekeeping in that it clearly excludes involvement in any type of peace enforcement.[32]

Even if there are no constitutional barriers, the new peacekeeping states may have difficulty rousing sufficient political support for dispatching troops halfway around the world to an unknown conflict. In dispatching the MNF to Haiti in 1994 the US Government struggled to convince public opinion and Congress of the rightness of the cause.

Pre-deployment briefing, training and preparation

The new peacekeepers, at least until very recently, joined the peacekeeping enterprise at a time when the UN was severely overstretched. The UN Secretariat has been faced with maintaining up to 18 missions in the field simultaneously, as well as preparing for new

[31] Kim, A. H. N., 'Japan and peacekeeping operations', *Military Review*, Apr. 1994, p. 28.
[32] Lintula, P., 'Finnish participation in peace-keeping operations', *International Peacekeeping*, Feb./May 1995, p. 44.

missions. In these circumstances there has been no time for strategic planning or training of contributing forces and little advice or assistance from the Secretariat in New York for the new contributors. Once the offer of a national contribution has been accepted, the new peacekeepers have been almost entirely on their own. This resulted, for instance, in civilian police arriving in Cambodia and Mozambique without the requisite language capabilities (English or French), driving skills or even police experience. Some contributors, like Ukraine, had barely established independent military forces before they were dispatched to participate in a very specialized form of military activity, requiring skills that can be the antithesis of those inculcated into military personnel. On the civilian side it has also been difficult to find personnel with the requisite qualifications and experience for the new peacekeeping tasks. In Cambodia UNTAC had great problems recruiting qualified, experienced international personnel to help monitor, control and supervise the workings of the State of Cambodia Government, as required under the 1991 Paris Peace Accords, and no time to train them itself.

Some last-minute pre-deployment training has been provided by the old peacekeepers (for instance, the Bulgarian battalion was given a month's training by Sweden before being dispatched to Cambodia) but it was often rushed and inadequate. The Bulgarian Parliament, in examining the failure of the Bulgarian contingent to perform well in Cambodia, concluded that the reasons were, along with the Khmer Rouge's 'negative attitude towards East Europeans', language difficulties and a lack of 'serious training'.[33] Little had apparently changed from the 'cottage industry' days of peacekeeping, when pre-deployment briefings were imparted by the Secretariat's tiny staff in a personalized, home-spun fashion and training was non-existent. Since the traditional operations tended to have simpler mandates, were much smaller and involved far fewer different nationalities and almost exclusively military personnel, this approach was adequate. In today's peacekeeping environment this is clearly insufficient.

In several cases of the 'old peacekeeping' the UN used experienced peacekeepers from existing operations as a core group around which a new mission would be built. In establishing UNIFIL in 1978 military

[33] Behar, N., 'Bulgarian peacekeeping prospects: new experience and new dilemmas', Paper presented to the SIPRI/Friedrich-Ebert-Stiftung Workshop on 'Challenges for the New Peacekeepers', Bonn, 21–22 Apr. 1994, pp. 5–6, unpublished manuscript.

personnel from UNTSO, UNDOF and UNEF II were transferred to Lebanon until they could be replaced by a permanent force.[34] New missions established since the end of the cold war have had to be built from the ground up, being so numerous and large that the use of personnel from existing missions has been impractical.

In the field I: growing complexity and danger

Upon arrival in the field the new peacekeepers have had to face increasing complexity in conditions that test the mettle of even the best-trained troops and civilian personnel. Some of the complexity has been planned, the result of ambitious peace-building operations as in El Salvador, Namibia and Cambodia. In other cases it evolved randomly and unexpectedly. In Bosnia and Herzegovina complexity came with deteriorating battlefield conditions, forcing ever more ingenious techniques on UNPROFOR to achieve delivery of humanitarian aid and inducing the Security Council to adopt over 100 resolutions and statements in its forlorn attempt to protect UN safe areas, dampen the conflict and achieve a lasting cease-fire and settlement.[35] As UN Secretary-General Boutros Boutros-Ghali has noted, 'peacekeeping has to be reinvented every day'.[36]

While not every post-cold war peacekeeping mission has included all of the following, the expanded repertoire of UN peacekeeping operations in 1993, for example, included: (*a*) election observation (Eritrea and Liberia) and organization (Cambodia); (*b*) humanitarian assistance and securing safe conditions for its delivery (Bosnia and Herzegovina, Somalia, Kurdish areas of Iraq); (*c*) observation and separation of combatants along a more or less demarcated boundary (Croatia, Kuwait–Iraq); (*d*) disarmament of military and paramilitary forces (Cambodia, Somalia and El Salvador); (*e*) promotion and protection of human rights (Cambodia and El Salvador); (*f*) mine clearance, training and mine awareness (Afghanistan and Cambodia); (*g*) military and police training (Cambodia and Haiti); (*h*) boundary

---

[34] Ghali, M., 'United Nations Interim Force in Lebanon', ed. W. J. Durch, *The Evolution of UN Peacekeeping: Case Studies and Comparative Analysis* (Henry L. Stimson Center: Washington, DC, 1993), p. 189.

[35] Akashi, Y., 'The role of the United Nations in the Balkans', *IBRU Boundary and Security Bulletin*, vol. 3, no. 2 (summer 1995), p. 45.

[36] UN, Report on the work of the Organization, Sep. 1993, UN document A/48/1 (advance version), p. 101.

demarcation (Kuwait–Iraq border); (*i*) civil administration (Cambodia); (*j*) provision of assistance to and repatriation of refugees (the former Yugoslavia, Cambodia and Somalia); (*k*) reconstruction and development (Cambodia and Somalia); and (*l*) maintenance of law and order (Cambodia and Somalia). Steven Ratner describes second-generation UN missions as combining the three roles of administrator, mediator and guarantor.[37]

Such complexity has troubled even experienced peacekeepers. As Canadian Major-General John MacInnis has noted, 'It is the aspect of complexity that poses challenges unthought of by peacekeepers only a few short years ago'.[38] In traditional peacekeeping operations, the observation of a cease-fire line or other boundary was the principal purpose of the mission, towards which all other activities could be directed. In the multi-purpose missions of today not only may the peacekeeper be faced with several objectives, but some of them may be in conflict with each other. In Cambodia it was alleged by human rights groups that the pursuit of human rights violators was subordinated to the goal of holding an election. In Somalia the goal of a peaceful settlement was subordinated to the quest for justice against those responsible for killing UN troops.

Such complexity has been compounded by the failings of the UN in planning and managing peacekeeping operations, both at UN headquarters and in the field. The UN Secretariat was caught unprepared for the vast expansion in the number and complexity of new missions since 1989. The ad hoc, amateurish, almost casual methods of the past simply could not keep pace, resulting in disorganization, mismanagement and waste. While such characteristics had always been present to some extent in UN operations, the scale and complexity of the new missions magnified the consequences. In simple border patrol operations where there was a peace to keep, it mattered little if administration was lax and late. In operations where the UN itself was running elections, overseeing governmental functions and protecting human rights it mattered a great deal. The new peacekeepers were thus thrown on to their own resources in ways undreamed of in the old peacekeeping.

[37] Ratner, S., *The New UN Peacekeeping* (Macmillan: London, 1995), pp. 44, 50.
[38] MacInnis, J. A., 'Peacekeeping and post-modern conflict: a soldier's view', *Mediterranean Quarterly*, vol. 6, no. 2 (spring 1995), p. 29.

An arduous new role in which peacekeepers have become involved for the first time is the delivery of humanitarian aid and the management of huge refugee movements—sometimes in the midst of continuing armed conflict in which civilian populations themselves have become targets of the fighting. As a British colonel with extensive experience in Bosnia and Herzegovina has noted: 'It wasn't a task the British Army had done before ... we were effectively sitting in the middle of somebody else's war' while trying to ensure the delivery of humanitarian aid.[39] While at home military forces are often called upon to assist national authorities in disaster relief, few forces have the experience or training to handle the sheer volume of humanitarian relief supplies to millions of starving people during a civil conflict, as in Somalia, or the mass movement of terrified refugees, as in Rwanda, Croatia and Bosnia and Herzegovina. In some cases, as in Bosnia and Herzegovina, civilians may be hostile to the presence of the peacekeepers, or alternatively, so dependent on them as to threaten to use obstructionist tactics or violence against them if they attempt to depart. Although the best militaries are well disciplined, organized and resourceful, few of the new peacekeepers will have the flexibility and sensitivity (not to mention training and equipment) for handling in a foreign environment such delicate situations as crowd control or intercommunal violence. While atrocities do occur in war, few military personnel are likely to be well prepared for witnessing, as impartial bystanders, massive human rights violations such as massacres of innocent civilians or for the accompanying sense of helplessness at being unable to do anything to stop them.[40]

Complexity is also introduced into the new peacekeeping by the multinational nature of the mission. UNTAC, the most international of any mission to date, along with its advance mission, UNAMIC, involved 34 nationalities among its military contingents and 32 among its civilian police. UNTAC's personnel in total were drawn from over 100 countries.[41] UNIFIL, in contrast, in all its 17 years had no more than 14 participating countries, most of which were experi-

---

[39] Duncan, A. D. (Col), 'Operating in Bosnia', *IBRU Boundary and Security Bulletin*, vol. 2, no. 3 (Oct. 1994), p. 47.

[40] British units in Bosnia and Herzegovina have psychiatric nurses available to help their troops cope with such experiences and their services are increasingly utilized. See Duncan (note 39), p. 56. Many of the new peacekeepers, however, have no such support systems.

[41] Findlay, T., *Cambodia: The Legacy and Lessons of UNTAC*, SIPRI Research Report no. 9 (Oxford University Press: Oxford, 1995), p. 27.

enced old peacekeepers.[42] New peacekeeping operations are therefore faced with multiple problems arising from a greater mix of capability, procedure, equipment, language, custom and ethos.

While in its older peacekeeping operations the UN could afford to be more selective in securing a judicious mix of capabilities and nationalities, today, when peacekeepers are in short supply for particular missions, there can be little choice but for the UN to accept whatever is offered. This has brought with it an inevitable lowering of standards. Sometimes the UN has been forced knowingly to accept contingents which were far from optimal in their training, experience or equipment. As the Secretary-General himself has lamented, 'You have to accept second-best and if not second-best you have to accept third-best' in the new peacekeeping.[43] In some cases corruption, human rights violations and loutish behaviour have distinguished such forces, rather than their contribution to peace. The deployment of such troops necessitates greater ability and adaptability on the part of each component and national contingent and heightened diplomatic skills on the part of the head of mission and the force commander. An added complication is that UN commanders do not have disciplinary authority over the foreign forces under their command and must rely on the goodwill of each contingent commander to enforce discipline.

The Secretary-General has also been obliged to accept contributions from the great powers and from states which have a direct interest in the outcome of the conflict, which was not the case in most missions during the old era of peacekeeping. This is most notable in the former Yugoslavia, where Germany, Russia, Turkey, the USA and Muslim states such as Malaysia have biases towards or against parties to the conflict. Such older missions as UNIFIL and UNFICYP involved former colonial powers with at least a residual interest in the conflict, France and Britain respectively, but their presence was less problematic since they were acceptable to all the parties concerned and provided the UN with indispensable local knowledge and specialized capabilities. Today the involvement of the permanent members of the Security Council raises the profile of most missions, increases their political sensitivity, encourages greater press attention and heightens

---

[42] UN, *The Blue Helmets* (note 26), pp. 427–28.
[43] Dowden, R., 'Boutros-Ghali accepts UN's limitations', *The Independent*, 27 Oct. 1994, p. 13.

expectations—perhaps offsetting the advantages of greater force capability, stronger political backing and heightened prestige.

A further complication in the new peacekeeping is a diminution of what Sashi Tharoor calls its 'United Nations-ness'.[44] Whereas peacekeeping missions during the cold war era were exclusively UN affairs, today the UN must share responsibilities in the field with regional organizations, as in Georgia where the CIS and OSCE are also operating, or, more problematically with a military alliance, as in the former Yugoslavia. The complexity of the 'dual-key' system for deciding when to use NATO air power in Bosnia and Herzegovina in furtherance of UN objectives was unprecedented in the history of UN peacekeeping. Similarly complex are arrangements in which the UN hands over authority and jurisdiction to a non-UN multilateral force, as in Somalia when UNOSOM I gave way to UNITAF, or when it takes over authority and jurisdiction from such a force, as at the end of UNITAF's mission and subsequently in Haiti. In the case of Iraq, UNIKOM was required to cooperate with and establish a peacekeeping operation on the border of a state which had been defeated in war by a UN-authorized coalition force. The new peacekeepers are thus required to coexist and cooperate with other entities in ways unheard of in the old peacekeeping—where the UN was usually the only player and perceived as benign by all sides.

Complexity is also introduced by the increasing civilianization of peacekeeping. There has been a civilian element in some traditional UN operations but they were present to administer operations rather than to participate in them.[45] Since the end of the cold war there have been several UN operations with large civilian components which have played an integral role in the peacekeeping mission and have sometimes been its *raison d'être*. This is true of the missions in Angola, Cambodia, El Salvador, Mozambique, Namibia, Somalia and Western Sahara. The addition of such substantial civilian components has de-emphasized the military character of peacekeeping, rendering the military component just one among many. Paradoxically it has also increased the range of tasks the military is called upon to perform, especially cooperative activities with civilian components, such as protection of and assistance with electoral activities. UNTAC was

---

[44] Tharoor, S., 'Peacekeeping: principles, problems, prospects', *Naval War College Review*, vol. 47, no. 2 (spring 1994), p. 4.
[45] Significant exceptions were ONUC and UNTEA.

the epitome of this trend.[46] It had seven components, only one of which was military. Other components had equally important roles and employed thousands of people. Alone, the Electoral Component's 62 000 employees, both local and international staff, dwarfed the military presence and a 3600-strong Civilian Police Component was also present. In addition there were several UN agencies such as the UN Development Programme (UNDP) or the UN High Commissioner for Refugees (UNHCR) and other foreign non-governmental organizations dealing with aid or human rights issues interacted with UNTAC. The local and international press were ubiquitous and influential, comprising yet another civilian element with which the new peacekeepers must increasingly deal.

Finally, complexity is increased because of the nature of the intra-state conflicts in which peacekeepers find themselves. Such conflicts usually involve multiple parties, the territory held by each party may be unclear and subject to rapid change, rogue elements within factions may adopt independent positions and take independent action and outside states may be involved in supporting one side or other. Civil wars are often literally life or death struggles in which the alternative to total control of state power is political or physical oblivion. The forces involved are also often better armed than in the past[47] and small ragtag armies may have more firepower than that available to the peacekeepers, even those from developed countries.

All these considerations make the new peacekeeping not only more complex but considerably more dangerous than the old. UN military casualties rose tenfold between 1991 and 1994, although the number of personnel deployed increased only eightfold.[48] Of the 33 fatalities between January 1992 and December 1993, '16 were killed in areas where no government authorities existed *de facto* or where such authorities were unable to maintain order and hence to discharge their responsibilities by protecting persons within their jurisdiction . . . 29 suffered from gunshot wounds, and there are grounds to believe that at least 6 were deliberately executed'.[49] In 1993 there were 11 fatalities among civilian peacekeeping staff.

---

[46] For detailed information on UNTAC, see Findlay (note 41), pp. 144–47.

[47] Martin, L., 'Peacekeeping as a growth industry', *National Interest*, summer 1993, p. 7.

[48] UN, Report of the Secretary-General on the work of the Organization, UN document A/49/1, 2 Sep. 1994, p. 58. It should be noted that the majority of casualties in peacekeeping missions are not caused by hostile fire. Road accidents account for a large proportion.

[49] UN, Note by the Secretary-General, UN document A/AC.242/1, 25 Mar. 1994.

One consequence of these trends is an increase in 'the normal tendency of contingents to seek guidance from their own capitals'.[50] This was seen at its worst in Somalia, where the Italians most famously, but also other contingents, sought instructions from home and then refused to act in accordance with the UN commander's directives. As experienced peacekeepers the Italians should have known better and their contingent commander was withdrawn at UN request. As Iqbal Riza notes, 'The anxieties of troop contributing countries for the safety of their troops are fully understandable, but it is evident that interference in operations only increases the danger to the personnel of the operation as a whole'.[51] In Cambodia Japanese Government concern over retaining tight control of its troops meant that every task, request or order had to be referred to Tokyo for clearance.[52]

A further consequence is disaffection at home with the peacekeeping mission, particularly in these days of rapid communication and saturation television coverage. Fatalities among the peacekeepers can trigger demands for withdrawal, debate about the nature of peacekeeping and calls for accountability. The reaction to the deaths of several Belgians in Rwanda was a case in point. Although Bulgarian opinion and the Bulgarian Parliament had been unanimous in supporting the dispatch of troops to Cambodia, the deaths of several of them brought strong pressure for their withdrawal.[53] Actual withdrawal is rare but does happen. New peacekeepers Tanzania and Uganda have withdrawn from ECOMOG in Liberia.[54] The best known withdrawal was that of the USA, followed by most of its Western allies, from Somalia after the killing of several of its troops in 1993 in Mogadishu.

A third consequence of the testing new environment is that it shows up more starkly the differences in the capabilities of different contingents. The better-equipped and trained troops, usually from Western states, are better able to defend themselves and to carry out other aspects of the new peacekeeping, whereas the less capable are both more vulnerable and less self-reliant. This mattered less in the less taxing environment of the old peacekeeping but in the new peace-

[50] Weiss, T. G., 'UN security forces in support of humane values', *Proceedings of the 88th Annual Meeting, American Society of International Law, 6–9 Apr. 1994* (American Society of International Law: New York, [1994]), p. 333.

[51] Riza, S. I., 'Parameters of UN peace-keeping', *RUSI Journal*, vol. 140, no. 3 (June 1995), p. 19.

[52] Kim, A. H. N., 'Japan and peacekeeping operations', *Military Review*, Apr. 1991, p. 28.

[53] Behar (note 33), p. 4.

[54] *International Peacekeeping News*, Mar. 1995, p. 4.

keeping it can strain relations between contingents, jeopardize the integrity of the force and even imperil aspects of the mission.

In the field II: challenges to traditional peacekeeping norms

Among the challenges that the new peacekeepers must cope with in second-generation missions are those that stretch to the limit the traditional peacekeeping norms relating to consent, impartiality and the use of force.

Consent of the parties

Consent may be shaky at the outset of a peacekeeping mission, perhaps because the parties have been inveigled against their will into a peace process or into agreeing to a UN presence, or it may degrade during a mission either because of the activities of the mission or because of factors beyond its control. In the worst case this leads to organized violence against peacekeepers. No UN peacekeeping deployment has yet been greeted with armed force (although the original deployment of UNMIH to Haiti sailed away after local thugs brandished weapons at them from the quay) or had to fight its way out (although fire was exchanged with Somalis during the withdrawal of UNOSOM II). During their deployment, however, many of the post-cold war peacekeeping operations have come under fire from one or more of the local belligerents. This can restrict forces' movements, complicate their tasks, especially those of the more vulnerable civilian components, and give the UN presence a garrison appearance and mentality.[55] Such an environment may undermine the morale of the mission and trigger calls for its withdrawal.

The principal challenge for peacekeepers in these circumstances is to attempt to establish or re-establish credibility and trust. The first requirement is to engage in persistent and painstaking negotiation with the parties. Since consent is weak, all manner of matters, from humanitarian aid convoy routes to the location of UN observer posts, must be negotiated and in many instances repeatedly renegotiated. The new peacekeepers also need to engage much more actively in so-called 'hearts and minds' campaigns to win over the civilian popula-

---

[55] This occurred during the first UN mission to Somalia, UNOSOM I, where 500 Pakistani peacekeepers huddled for months at Mogadishu airport, afraid to venture out.

tion and in 'civil information' campaigns designed to explain their presence. Lieutenant-General John Sanderson, the UNTAC force commander, claims that the success of his mission was due to its ability to 'forge an alliance' with the Cambodian people against those parties seeking to undermine the peace process and hence to conduct a free and fair election and democratic transfer of power.[56]

In circumstances of doubtful or eroding consent the military component also needs to be better trained and equipped to defend itself and its mission (including the usually substantial civilian presence) and be at a higher stage of readiness and alert than in a situation of assured consent. The standard of such elements as communications and command and control also needs to be higher. UN command and control arrangements have traditionally been complicated by language problems, incompatible equipment and procedures, the lack of common training and staff structures and the need for geographical balance among participating states. They also suffer from multiple chains of command both in the theatre and between the military and civilian sides of the UN.

An enhanced military capability may, depending on circumstances and the local culture, afford peacekeepers more authority and prestige. As Colonel Alistair Duncan has noted of Bosnia and Herzegovina: 'Very sadly the rule of the gun is what matters . . . the man with the AK-47 is a big man. I had clout because with 56 Warriors [a tracked infantry combat vehicle] I was considered to be the most powerful man in Central Bosnia'.[57] New peacekeepers from poorer, developing states will be more vulnerable in such situations unless provided with adequate protective equipment.

The most feared scenario is a complete loss of consent. This is most likely to occur after the UN has attempted punitive or retaliatory action against one of the parties as a result of non-cooperation or violation of agreements or international law. Following the NATO bombing of Bosnian Serb ammunition dumps near Pale in June 1995, after the Serbs refused to return heavy weapons seized from UN collection points, the Bosnian Serb leadership declared that all agreements with the UN were null and void, thereby explicitly withdrawing consent for the presence and activities of UNPROFOR. This was followed by the

[56] Sanderson, J. M. (Lt-Gen.), 'A review of peacekeeping operations', Paper presented to the Pacific Armies Management Seminar (PAMS) XVIII Conference, Dacca, Jan. 1994, p. 14.
[57] Duncan (note 39), p. 54.

taking hostage of hundreds of UNPROFOR observers and troops. Such situations clearly place a peacekeeping mission in an impossible situation: with consent withdrawn the very vulnerability that is a condition of peacekeeping forces' succeeding permits their capture and use as political pawns.

When consent breaks down altogether the stark choices for the peacekeepers are then to withdraw, soldier on or convert to peace enforcement. While the transition from consent-based peacekeeping to consent-less peace enforcement is difficult, it is not impossible, as demonstrated by UNPROFOR in August 1995. It must, however, be well planned, be deliberate (rather than the result of 'mission creep') and be accompanied by the necessary changes in capability, mandate and commitment of force.

Impartiality

A second key tenet of traditional peacekeeping under challenge is the maintenance of an impartial, non-discriminatory stance towards all the parties to a conflict. Abandonment of impartiality, whether deliberate or inadvertent, runs the risk of turning the peacekeeping force into an enemy of one or more of the parties. Safeguarding the impartiality of the mission will be a constant preoccupation in situations where consent is fragile and will require some fine judgement on the part of the mission commander. A traditional UN border monitoring operation can proceed with its duties relatively unaffected by internal instability within a state, but a peacekeeping force in the midst of an intra-state conflict is invariably caught up in events and may through its actions pivotally affect their outcome.[58] For instance, if only one party is breaking a cease-fire, impartiality is virtually impossible because UN forces may have to adopt defensive measures to protect themselves against that party. Even though a warring party has brought discrimination on itself it will accuse the UN of bias. The preferred situation may be that in Cambodia, where all parties accused the UN of partiality.

For the new peacekeepers the implications of the doctrine of impartiality include a need for greater care, awareness and sophistication in dealing with the parties. The new peacekeepers' roles of administrator, arbitrator and enforcer as well as keeper of the peace require

[58] James, A., 'A review of UN peacekeeping', *Internationale Spectator*, vol. 18, no. 11 (Nov. 1993), p. 632.

special training in diplomacy, conflict resolution, mediation and other fuctions, which is not normally imparted to military personnel or even most civilian personnel recruited to UN missions.

Use of force

One of the main bones of contention between the old and new peace-keepers has been their differing attitudes to the use of military force. Traditionalists favoured persisting with the 'Scandinavian model' of strict adherence to the tried and true principles of peacekeeping, patient persuasion and negotiation and the minimum use of force, even in self-defence. Britain, relatively new to peacekeeping, recommended a 'wider peacekeeping' that was more robust but which basically retained the traditional peacekeeping ethos and practices. Some of the new peacekeepers, most notably the USA, supported by France, and even developing states like Malaysia on various occasions advocated greater use of force.

Greater use of force runs the risk of transforming a UN mission from peacekeeping to peace enforcement, either suddenly or through mission creep. As well as being dangerous to the forces on the ground, such a development is also fundamentally unfair to those nations which have contributed in good faith to what they supposed was a peacekeeping mission, and especially unfair to smaller contributors which usually have no say in such transformations unless they happen to be non-permanent members of the Security Council at the time. The withdrawal of their contingents may be not only politically embarrassing to effect but also physically impossible without the assistance of more powerful states. The fate of the Bangladeshi contingent trapped in Bihac in early 1995 is one example. Not only were they poorly equipped to defend themselves, being armed only with rifles, but they had not anticipated being in a situation of virtual all-out war in which withdrawal was impossible. In Somalia an even worse situation occurred when the Western states largely abandoned the UN mission to the non-Western contingents such as Egypt, India, Pakistan and Zimbabwe. While some of the contingents left behind were experienced old peacekeepers, the spectacle of the more technologically sophisticated and militarily capable states forsaking the mission after having led it into peace enforcement did nothing to promote enthusiasm for the new peacekeeping and made it more difficult to recruit contributors for future missions such as that in Rwanda.

After the Somalia débâcle a consensus appeared to emerge among the UN, major troop contributors like the UK and the USA and new and old peacekeepers alike that, apart from self-defence or defence of the mission, military force can only be used for enforcement purposes, if at all, at a low tactical level, if a peacekeeping mission is not to be fatally jeopardized. It is now recognized that peace enforcement operations require a vastly different array of forces, command and control arrangements, military doctrine and political underpinning. The US Army's field manual on peace operations now advises that:

The proper use of force is critical in a peace operation. The use of force to attain a short-term tactical success could lead to a long-term strategic failure. The use of force may affect other aspects of the operation. The use of force may attract a response in kind, heighten tension, polarize public opinion against the operation and participants, foreclose negotiating opportunities, prejudice the perceived impartiality of the peace operation force, and escalate the overall level of violence . . . In [peacekeeping], commanders should regard the use of force as a last resort.[59]

The UN Commission of Enquiry into the events in Mogadishu recommended that the UN 'refrain from undertaking further peace enforcement actions within the internal conflicts of states',[60] but that if peace enforcement was nevertheless undertaken the mandate of the force 'should be limited to specific objectives and the use of force should be applied as the ultimate means after all peaceful remedies have been exhausted'. Increased use of preventive diplomacy, peace building and emergency assistance was recommended.

UNPROFOR's at times surreal relationship with all the warring parties in the former Yugoslavia combined an enforcement role (with the assistance of NATO) with consent-based humanitarian activities, a mix that ultimately proved untenable. It produced a confusing operational environment for the new peacekeepers, where consent was present one day and not the next, in one situation and not another. However, the handling of the joint NATO/UNPROFOR peace enforcement bombing campaign against the Bosnian Serbs in August

[59] US Department of the Army Headquarters, *Peace Operations*, Field Manual 100–23, Dec. 1994, pp. 33–34.

[60] UN, Report of the Commission of Inquiry established pursuant to Security Council Resolution 885 (1993) to investigate armed attacks on UNOSOM II personnel which led to casualties among them, New York, 24 Feb. 1994, appended to UN, Note by the Secretary-General, 1 June 1994 (note 30), p. 48.

1995, preceded by the deployment of a well-equipped Rapid Reaction Force and the withdrawal of peacekeepers to safe positions, indicated that the lessons of Somalia had been belatedly learned.

Even if the new peacekeepers avoid being drawn into peace enforcement, the chances of them being required to use force, if only in self-defence and defence of their mission, are higher than they were in the old peacekeeping.

Even when force is strictly limited to self-defence and not extended to the defence of the mission there may be ambiguities. Rules of engagement (ROEs) may lack detail, change over time or vary between national contingents. For instance, the right to self-defence may or may not, in the interpretation of a particular commander, include the right to a pre-emptive attack if peacekeepers believe a strike against them is imminent. In Cambodia, for example, the Dutch and French battalions were using completely different ROEs from those of the Bangladeshis, Bulgarians and Indonesians. This runs the risk of factional forces playing off one battalion against another, taking advantage of the less robust. A similar problem occurred in Somalia, where the Italians were much more willing than US forces to negotiate rather than respond aggressively to provocation. Even the best ROEs will not cover all situations.

The peacekeeper's right to protect the peace process is also ambiguous and potentially open-ended. In regard to Rwanda it was argued by some that UNAMIR's forces should have positioned themselves between the Hutu killers and their victims and that any use of force which resulted could have been justified on the grounds of 'defending the mission'. Others regard the protection of populations in danger as going beyond protecting the mission unless specified in the mission mandate.

Financial implications

The boom in peacekeeping since the end of the cold war has plunged the UN into debt. Financial support for peacekeeping operations has lagged behind political support despite the fact that assessed contributions are a legal obligation of member states.[61] As of 31 May 1995

---

[61] The funding for all but 2 peacekeeping operations, UNTSO and UNMOGIP, comes from special assessments of member states, rather than from the UN regular budget. A third mission, UNFICYP, is partly funded by voluntary contributions.

outstanding assessments to the UN for peacekeeping amounted to $1.03 billion.[62] This has affected the new peacekeepers in two ways.

First, the UN has found it increasingly difficult to reimburse contributors for their peacekeeping costs. By the end of 1995 it is estimated that unpaid reimbursements to troop contributors and payments for contingent-owned equipment are likely to reach $1 billion.[63] Essentially this is an enforced loan to the UN from member states. Like Tunisia, several new peacekeepers have expressed difficulties about their future participation unless they are compensated more readily and in full.

In the old peacekeeping there were also financial difficulties at times and reimbursement was not always prompt, but most of the participants were wealthy developed states which were able to absorb costs. Today the sums involved are far greater and the majority of the new peacekeepers are less well endowed developing states which have been encouraged to contribute to peacekeeping to spread the international burden. Without significant reforms in this area the UN will be unable to sustain the goodwill of the new peacekeepers, especially those from the developing world.

Second, the ballooning peacekeeping bill has thrown an additional financial burden on states because their assessed contributions have also increased. Even New Zealand, a relatively wealthy contributor, has seen its peacekeeping assessment rise from $1 million per year in the 1980s to $16 million in 1995.[64] For the largest financial contributor, the USA, the burden has become so great that it is unilaterally dropping its level of support from about 30 per cent to 25 per cent from October 1995 onwards. While in some cases there may be a balance between what a particular state owes the UN and what the UN owes it, the position for others, particularly those which pay their UN dues in full and on time and are then not reimbursed for their substantial peacekeeping contributions, will be inequitable.

[62] UN, Press Release DH/1889, 9 May 1995, p. 4.

[63] UN, Report of the Secretary-General on the work of the Organization, UN document A/50/1 (note 7), p. 21.

[64] 'New Zealand in the Security Council 1993–94' (note 2), p. 13.

V. Conclusion

With several of the largest and most ambitious post-cold war missions now ended (notably those in Cambodia, El Salvador, Mozambique and Somalia) and no major ones on the horizon, the heyday of peace-keeping may have already passed. The UN, with a mixed record of success and failure and plagued by staggering financial deficits, is facing a period of consolidation and reconsideration of its peacekeeping activities.

None the less peacekeeping has sufficiently proved its worth when done properly to have confirmed its place as a primary tool of conflict prevention, management and resolution in certain circumstances. It is therefore likely to remain in the UN repertoire for the foreseeable future. There are enough unattended conflicts in Africa and the former Soviet republics alone to keep peacekeepers occupied well into the next century. The UN is undertaking a serious effort to reform its peacekeeping capabilities both at UN headquarters and in the field. The Department of Peace-keeping Operations has been reorganized and expanded, a Situation Room now operates 24 hours a day, and a Standby Forces Arrangement has been initiated. Better planning, training, command and control arrangements and management are in prospect. However, financial constraints and problems attendant on wider systemic reform of the UN will continue to be limiting factors.[65]

Even if major developments occur, such as the UN establishing its own rapid reaction force or other type of military capability, the world body and other international organizations which engage in peace-keeping will still need the contribution of the new peacekeepers. While the UN should be strongly enjoined and assisted to improve its own capacities further, the enhancement and augmentation of national efforts, particularly those of the new peacekeepers, will be just as important to the future of the new peacekeeping.

[65] For an annual account of UN peacekeeping gnerally and of reform efforts in particular, see Findlay, T., 'Multinational conflict prevention, management and resolution', *SIPRI Yearbook 1994* (note 29), pp. 13–80; Findlay, T., 'Armed conflict prevention, management and resolution', *SIPRI Yearbook 1995: Armaments, Disarmament and International Security* (Oxford University Press: Oxford, 1995), pp. 37–116; and Findlay, T., 'Armed conflict prevention, management and resolution', *SIPRI Yearbook 1996: Armaments, Disarmament and International Security* (Oxford University Press: Oxford, 1996, forthcoming).

2. Germany

Hans-Georg Ehrhart

I. Introduction

As a major economic power and reunified sovereign state, Germany would seem at first glance to have no problem in contributing to UN peacekeeping operations. The evolution of Germany as a new peace-keeper has, however, to be set in the wider context of a restructuring of the international environment and a difficult, multi-layered domestic debate.[1] In this chapter emphasis is placed on the internal German debate because its outcome will influence not only the future international role of the new Germany but also its political identity. After a historical glance at the relationship between the 'old' Germany—comprising the former German Democratic Republic (GDR) and the Federal Republic of Germany (FRG)—and the UN, more recent political developments in the new united Germany are analysed on the levels of government, the political parties, the military and society. It will be argued that, although opinion on the future role of Germany is in transition at all levels of society, the new Germany still has a long way to go in overcoming various internal obstacles to a significantly stronger engagement in UN missions. This learning process will be considerably influenced both by its own experience as a new peace-keeper and by the evolution of multilateral thinking about the entire concept of peacekeeping.

II. The legacy of German history

The relationship between Germany and the UN was determined by the former's role in World War II and in the cold war. The immediate motivation for founding the UN was the Allied effort against Germany and the other Axis powers and the need for a new and peaceful world order.

---

[1] See, for example, Kühne, W. (ed.), *Blauhelme in einer turbulenten Welt* [Blue helmets in a turbulent world] (Nomos: Baden-Baden, 1993) (in German); and Ehrhart, H.-G. and Ehrhart, W., 'L'Allemagne et l'ONU' [Germany and the United Nations], *Politique Étrangère*, no. 3 (1993), pp. 673–85 (in French).

This situation is illustrated by the 'enemy state' clauses. In accordance with Article 53.2 of the UN Charter, the term 'enemy state' applied to any state which during World War II was an enemy of any signatory of the Charter. These clauses finally became de facto obsolete with the signing of the treaty of 12 August 1970 between the FRG and the USSR on the inviolability of the existing borders in Europe and the acceptance of the two German states as members of the United Nations in 1973.

The division of Germany also constituted a special factor. The two German states could only become members of the UN by agreement with the permanent members of the Security Council and with one another. In the 1950s and 1960s the FRG had insisted, with support from the Western Allies, on the sole right to represent Germany. It was the *Ostpolitik* of the former Chancellor of the FRG, Willy Brandt, and the political *modus vivendi* established in the Treaty on Basic Relations concluded in 1972 between the FRG and GDR which paved the way for UN membership for both. In connection with the Treaty the two German states agreed in an exchange of letters of 8 November 1972 that they would apply for UN membership at about the same time.

Once UN membership had been achieved, the 'German Question' was no longer an issue at the UN and the 'Berlin Question' became no more of an issue than the question of Germany's division. For the GDR, the Treaty on Basic Relations codified the existence of two states in Germany. For the Federal Republic, the UN was not an appropriate forum for dealing with the German Question. Both attributed greater importance to the question of European security than to German unity. As a result, both restricted themselves to presenting their policy on the issue in the general debate held by the General Assembly each year. In this regard the UN did not play as important a role for the two German states as did their respective alliances and the Conference on Security and Co-operation in Europe (CSCE).[2]

The GDR did not involve itself in UN peacekeeping activities except for sending a small group of police monitors to UNTAG in Namibia in 1989. Following the example of the USSR, it refused to

[2] Bruns, W., *Die Uneinigen in den Vereinten Nationen, Bundesrepublik Deutschland und DDR in der UNO* [The disunited in the United Nations: the FRG and the GDR in the UN] (Verlag Wissenschaft und Politik: Cologne, 1980) (in German). On 1 Jan. 1995 the CSCE became the Organization for Security and Co-operation in Europe (OSCE).

pay its share of the costs.[3] Before gaining UN membership, the FRG provided voluntary financial contributions to UNFICYP in 1967. In the 1970s it supported the UN 'blue helmets' in monitoring the cease-fire between Israel and Egypt in 1973 (UNEF II) and in Lebanon in 1978 (UNIFIL) by providing equipment and transport; and in 1989 it became involved in UN peacekeeping missions in UNTAG and in Central America (ONUCA), this time involving the deployment of civilian personnel.

Hence, while the FRG became indirectly engaged in UN peacekeeping missions, it did not cross the threshold of involving military personnel.

III. The incremental approach of the new Germany

Since unification Germany has faced the challenge of redefining its political priorities and goals in a rapidly evolving security environment. With the UN now perceived as an important decision-making body on security issues, Germany has been increasingly involved in UN peace missions, not all of them involving peacekeeping as traditionally understood. Whereas support for MINURSO and UNMIH in Haiti involved civilian personnel, in other cases German military personnel were involved for the first time, initially in the framework of humanitarian measures but then also in connection with military activities.[4]

1. In spring 1991 Germany supplied food, emergency shelter and field hospitals to Kurdish refugees in eastern Turkey and western Iran on the basis of Security Council Resolution 688. With nearly 2000 soldiers involved, this was at the time the largest humanitarian mission ever undertaken by the Bundeswehr.

2. After Operation Desert Storm in 1991 the government responded to a request of the USA and the UN to support the international mine-clearing action in the Persian Gulf. Approximately 2700 German troops were involved, of whom more than 700 were conscripts.

3. Since August 1991 Germany has assigned one diplomat from the Foreign Ministry, nine experts from the Defence Ministry and nearly

---

[3] The Soviet Union changed its position in 1987. See Gorbachev, M., *Pravda*, 17 Sep. 1987 (in Russian), excerpted in *Europa-Archiv*, no. 24 (1987), pp. D 656–62 (in German).

[4] For the official record see Bundesministerium der Verteidigung, *Weißbuch 1994* [White Book 1994] (Presse- und Informationsamt der Bundesregierung: Bonn, 1994), pp. 70–74.

50 soldiers, airmen and ground personnel to UNSCOM. The official interpretation is that this is not a special military operation, but a disarmament-related mission.

4. In November 1991 Germany provided six doctors and nine Federal Armed Forces paramedics for UNAMIC. In April 1992 the government assigned approximately 150 Federal Armed Forces physicians and paramedics as well as 75 Federal Border Guard officials to UNTAC. This was the first time that members of the German armed forces were involved in a UN peacekeeping mission. Shortly before the scheduled end of the UNTAC mission in November 1993 they suffered their first casualty.

5. Between August 1992 and March 1993 the German Air Force flew 655 flights which transported about 6000 tons of humanitarian relief supplies to Somalia. In December 1992 the government offered to provide the UN with supply and transport exclusively for use in 'pacified areas' of Somalia. These flights in support of UNOSOM I were considered to be humanitarian, not military.

6. Thus far, for constitutional and historical reasons, Germany has not contributed military ground personnel to UNPROFOR.[5] However, it is involved in monitoring the economic embargo against the rump Yugoslav state (Serbia and Montenegro) in the Adriatic (since June 1992) and on the Danube (since April 1993), in monitoring the no-fly zone over Bosnia and Herzegovina (since October 1992) and in the international airlift there (since July 1992). These missions are interpreted by the government as humanitarian rather than military.

7. On 2 April 1993 the government decided not to withdraw German fire control officers from the multinational crew of the NATO airborne warning and control system (AWACS) squadron whose command and control systems were about to be used to assist the military enforcement of the no-fly zone over Bosnia and Herzegovina authorized by the UN Security Council. Hence, since April 1993, with the tentative approval of the Federal Constitutional Court,[6] German soldiers have been officially involved in a military enforcement mission for the first time since World War II.

---

[5] During World War II Germany, together with Italy, invaded Yugoslavia, annexed parts of Slovenia, occupied parts of Serbia, Montenegro and Macedonia, and installed in the rest of Yugoslavia the fascist Ustasha regime of Croatia as a satellite state of Nazi Germany.
[6] See section V in this chapter.

IV. Somalia: a turning-point

At the end of April 1993, in response to a request by UN Secretary-General Boutros Boutros-Ghali, the German Government decided to make available an armed forces contingent consisting of 1640 men for transport, logistic and engineering work in connection with UNOSOM II in Somalia. The government insisted that the German forces be stationed in a pacified area and not be used in a combat role. The Security Council tailored Resolution 814 of 26 March 1993 accordingly. Part A of the resolution mentions humanitarian tasks such as protection of the distribution of relief supplies, repatriation of refugees and support of economic reconstruction, while part B allows enforcement actions under Chapter VII of the UN Charter. This made it possible for the German Government to interpret the participation of a Bundeswehr battalion in UNOSOM II as being part of a peacekeeping mission under Chapter VI of the UN Charter, even though UNOSOM as a whole could be interpreted as a peace enforcement operation.[7] The government was driven by two motives. First, it wanted to present the German public with a *fait accompli*. Second, to back its campaign for a permanent seat on the UN Security Council it wished to demonstrate Germany's political willingness and military capability to participate in any kind of international activity authorized by the Council.[8]

At the end of July 1993 the main German contingent arrived in Belet Uen. Only three months later Defence Minister Volker Rühe announced that Germany's contingent might be gradually withdrawn by April 1994.[9] Officially this was ascribed to the diversion of the Indian contingent, which was to have been supported by the German transport unit and which never arrived in Belet Uen. The real reason was the withdrawal of US and most other Western forces following the tragic failure of UNOSOM's US-dominated policy, which led to scores of UN casualties, including 18 American deaths. Following the US lead the last German soldier left Somalia on 28 February 1994.

The first major out-of-area mission of the German armed forces since World War II began not only on the shaky basis of an unclear

[7] Nass, M., 'Blauhelme für Anfänger' [Blue helmets for beginners], *Die Zeit*, 23 Apr. 1993 (in German).

[8] Wagner, W., 'Abenteuer Somalia' [The Somalia adventure], *Europa-Archiv*, no. 6 (1994), pp. 151–60 (in German).

[9] 'Germany may quit Somalia by April', *International Herald Tribune*, 18 Oct. 1993.

UN mandate but also amid a major domestic political controversy in Germany over its future role in international conflict management.[10]

At the end of the 1970s there had already been a brief controversy over the involvement of the German armed forces in UN peace missions. Advocates of German involvement based their arguments on Germany's increased weight in foreign policy matters, its reputation and its greater share of responsibility for resolving international conflicts. The Foreign Ministry took a negative stance on constitutional grounds,[11] referring to Article 87a of the German Constitution of 1949, according to which armed forces are to be built up 'for defence purposes' and 'may only be used to the extent explicitly permitted' by the constitution. In addition to the political arguments they presented, the advocates of involvement also cited Article 24 of the constitution, which permits Germany to 'enter a system of mutual collective security for the purpose of preserving peace'. In 1982 the Federal Security Council[12] reaffirmed that the constitution forbids out-of-area use of German forces. During the Persian Gulf War (1990–91) Germany supported the international coalition against Iraq with considerable financial, logistical, medical and military assistance, but officially without military personnel in the war zone.[13] This was done on the basis that the operation had been authorized by the UN Security Council. The government has thus followed a step-by-step approach, extending the German engagement in practice while officially defending the need to amend the constitution.

In 1991 Foreign Minister Hans-Dietrich Genscher declared in a statement to the 46th session of the UN General Assembly that a united Germany would assume all rights and obligations under the UN Charter, including collective security measures, 'also with our armed forces. We want to change our constitution for this purpose'.[14]

[10] Kennan, G. F., 'Into Somalia: a dreadful error of American policy', *International Herald Tribune*, 1 Oct. 1993; and Bertram, B., 'Weg mit Schaden?' [Journey with damage?], *Die Zeit*, 19 Nov. 1993 (in German).

[11] Deutscher Bundestag, *Protokolle*, no. 12/151, p. 12937 (B).

[12] The Federal Security Council is a special cabinet committee responsible for security matters, comprising the Chancellor and the Ministers of Defence, Justice, Foreign Affairs, the Interior, the Economy and Finance.

[13] The Ministry of Defence indirectly confirmed reports alleging that German soldiers were involved in AWACS missions in 1991 during the Persian Gulf War. See 'AWACs-Besatzung im Golf-Krieg' [AWACS crew in the Gulf War], *Süddeutsche Zeitung*, 21 Jan. 1993 (in German).

[14] Speech by Foreign Minister Genscher to the 46th session of the UN General Assembly, 25 Sep. 1991. See *Vereinte Nationen*, no. 5 (1991), pp. 168–71 (in German).

Speaking to the same forum a year later, the new Foreign Minister, Klaus Kinkel, called for the establishment of an effective system of collective security within the UN and CSCE frameworks. He affirmed Germany's intention to create the constitutional prerequisites 'for our armed forces to be placed at the disposal of the United Nations for peacekeeping and peace-restoring missions after approval by the Bundestag'. Kinkel said that Germany did not want a gap to develop between its verbal commitment to peace and human rights and its active commitment. He also made an initial reference to the question of a permanent seat for Germany on the UN Security Council by stating that Germany would not take the initiative, but would state its claim if and when specific plans were to be made to change the composition of the Security Council.[15] Nine months later the government, responding to an official question of the Secretary-General, declared its preparedness to assume the responsibilities of permanent membership of the Security Council.[16] Although Germany was backed in principle by the five permanent members, France, the UK and the USA (Germany's closest allies) emphasized that new members would be expected to play an active role in global security activities.[17]

The UN Secretary-General tried several times to seek German commitment to greater international engagement, while being fully aware of the complicated internal situation of the new Germany. In an interview given to a German weekly he rejected explicitly any question of Germany providing soldiers for UN enforcement missions, emphasizing that UN activities comprise other tasks and that it is the prerogative of each country to decide what it offers the UN.[18] During a visit to Bonn in April 1994 he argued in favour of the creation of a UN stand-by peacekeeping force, the German share of which should not

[15] Speech by Foreign Minister Kinkel to the 47th session of the UN General Assembly, 23 Sep. 1992. See Press and Information Office of the Federal Government, *Bulletin*, no. 101 (25 Sep. 1992), pp. 1949–53 (in German).

[16] *Frankfurter Allgemeine Zeitung*, 2 July 1993 (in German). See also 'Farewell to the Genscher era' [interview with Klaus Kinkel], *Süddeutsche Zeitung*, 13 May 1993; and Press and Information Office of the Federal Government, *Bulletin*, no. 79 (30 Sep. 1993), pp. 913–17 (in German).

[17] For the text of the statements, see *Europa-Archiv*, no. 19 (1993), pp. D385–87, D390–93 (in German).

[18] 'Die Hand am Drücker' [The hand on the trigger], *Die Woche*, 17 Feb. 1994 (in German).

exceed 1 per cent of its armed forces, approximately 3000 troops.[19] Hence the Secretary-General as well as Germany's closest allies increased the pressure on Germany to resolve its internal debate on its future international role and responsibilities.

V. The Constitutional Court's decision

On the juridical level the internal debate was closed by the ruling of the Federal Constitutional Court in July 1994.[20] It declared constitutional the participation of Germany in all kinds of crisis and peace operations, including peace enforcement, subject to the consent of a majority of the lower house of parliament, the Bundestag. At a special session on 22 July 1994 the latter gave *ex post facto* approval to the participation of the Bundeswehr in the UN-mandated NATO and Western European Union (WEU) missions in the former Yugoslavia.

While emphasizing that the promise given to the UN General Assembly in 1991 by his predecessor, Hans-Dietrich Genscher, had been kept, Foreign Minister Kinkel pledged continuing respect for the post-war German culture of restraint.[21] He specifically mentioned Germany's prudence regarding the use of military means, which was a product of the lessons of German history, the need for priority to be given to conflict prevention and the fact that the Bundeswehr was not yet prepared for participating in international peace missions in distant areas. Cautioning that Germany's partners should not make excessive demands on it and that each case had to be studied carefully, Kinkel formulated principles and questions which will be of importance in future German decision making:

1. German participation in international peace missions must be in accordance with international law.

2. Germany will never engage in peace missions alone, but only in multilateral operations, primarily in the framework of existing international institutions such as the UN, the OSCE, NATO and the WEU.

---

[19] 'Boutros-Ghali: Die Vereinten Nationen brauchen jederzeit verfügbare Streitkräfte' [Boutros-Ghali: The United Nations need standby forces], *Frankfurter Allgemeine Zeitung*, 11 Apr. 1994 (in German).

[20] Bundesverfassungsgericht, 2 BvE 3/92, 2 BvE 5/93, 2 BvE 7/93, 2 BvE 8/93, pronounced on 12 July 1994 (in German).

[21] Kinkel, K. 'Peacekeeping missions: Germany can now play its part', *NATO Review*, vol. 42, no. 5 (Oct. 1994), pp. 3–7.

3. The following questions must be answered in a satisfactory way. Is there a clear mandate? Is the proposed military action sensibly embedded in a comprehensive political conception of conflict resolution? Is there a reasonable likelihood of the mission succeeding? Is there a reasonable balance between the goal sought and the potential losses that might be incurred? Are there clear criteria for assessing success so that the mission can be terminated in a timely fashion? Do contingency plans exist in case it is not as successful as hoped?

4. The more probable combat missions are, the more compelling must be the reasons for German participation.

5. In addition to parliamentary approval and an assessment of the risks and possible consequences of a military mission out-of-area, an all-party consensus should be sought.

6. German participation should not have an escalatory effect on the conflict, which could be the case in areas where special animosities still exist because of German occupation during World War II: 'For this reason the Federal Government rejects the direct participation of German troops in peace missions in the former Yugoslavia'.[22]

Following the ruling of the Federal Constitutional Court, which widened the German foreign policy options from a legal point of view, decisions on actual participation now lie with the politicians. The criteria defined by the Foreign Minister underline Germany's still cautious approach. None the less, events such as NATO's request in December 1994 for German Tornado aircraft[23] to participate in the NATO operation in the former Yugoslavia, the request some days later for a German contribution in case NATO was required to protect UNPROFOR's withdrawal,[24] and the debate on the extent and nature of Germany's support for the new Rapid Reaction Force (RRF) in

[22] Kinkel (note 21), p. 7.

[23] Electronic combat and reconnaissance aircraft (ECRs). At first, the Federal Government avoided a decision by declaring the NATO request 'informal'. See *Frankfurter Allgemeine Zeitung*, 8 Dec. 1994 (in German).

[24] In this case the government publicly pursued a delaying tactic, giving assurances that Germany would make a contribution while cautioning that a concrete decision would have to be taken in each situation. See 'Die SPD zu Gesprächen über einen deutschen Beitrag bereit' [SPD ready for talks on a German contribution], *Frankfurter Allgemeine Zeitung*, 16 Dec. 1994 (in German). At the same time the Defence Ministry compiled a list for NATO contingency planning which earmarked 70 officers for the UN/NATO headquarters in Kieseljak near Sarajevo, maritime transport and mine clearing capacities, Tornado ECRs, additional Transall airlift capacities and army logistics and paramedic units. See Junacker, M., 'Bonner Plan: 70 deutsche Uffiziere nach Bosnien' [The Bonn plan: 70 German officers to Bosnia], *Welt am Sonntag*, 18 Dec. 1994 (in German).

Bosnia and Herzegovina all indicate that Germany will be confronted with growing demands for its participation in peace operations.

In the latter case, the government gave approval on 26 June 1995 to the Bundeswehr protecting and supporting the RRF by providing air transport capacity for the transport of peacekeeping forces outside the borders of Bosnia and Herzegovina, by dispatching paramedics to Croatia and staff personnel to the international headquarters in Italy and Croatia and by participating in NATO's close air support activities.[25] Following this decision, approved by the Bundestag with the votes of the ruling parties and with 45 votes of the opposition just four days later, the Bundeswehr for the first time was officially deployed in a combat theatre.[26] The fact that the government restricted the mission of the Tornados—apart from contingency planning for a complete withdrawal of UNPROFOR and UNCRO—to the protection of the RRF, its insistence that it is their task to enforce the no-fly zone and its refusal to commit ground forces to Bosnia and Herzegovina all demonstrate its continuing caution.[27]

Thus the political debate in Germany over its role in the building of a new security order has only just begun.

VI. The political parties

While there is broad consensus in the Bundestag that Germany should not stand aside while the UN assumes growing global burdens, there has been a dispute at the constitutional level as to whether or not the

[25] Germany has provided 500 paramedics, 8 Tornado ECRs to neutralize Bosnian Serb missiles, 6 Tornado ECRs for infrared reconnaissance, 2 Breguet Atlantic reconnaissance planes, 12 Transall transport planes and 1000 staff and logistic personnel. See 'Der Bonner Regierungsbeschluss zur Unterstützung der Blauhelm-Soldaten in Bosnien' [The Bonn government decision to support the blue helmets in Bosnia], *Frankfurter Rundschau*, 27 June 1995 (in German).

[26] 'Bundestag stimmt Einsatz von Tornados zu' [Bundestag approves mission of Tornados], *Süddeutsche Zeitung*, 1–2 July 1995 (in German).

[27] As early as Dec. 1994 the UN Secretary-General had assured Chancellor Helmut Kohl that German Tornados would not be requested for use in implementing existing UN mandates. This restriction is monitored by a German Air Force General in Italy who examines every request for German Tornados to check its compatability with the 2 approved missions, i.e., the protection of the RRF and of a complete withdrawal of the 'blue helmets'. See Kornelius, S., 'Eingreifstruppe bringt Bonn in ein Dilemma' [Reaction Force puts Bonn in a dilemma], *Süddeutsche Zeitung*, 17 June 1995 (in German); and 'Die Abstimmung über den Bosnien-Einsatz wird zur Zerreißprobe für die SPD' [The vote on the Bosnia mission is becoming a tension test for the SPD], *Frankfurter Allgeimeine Zeitung*, 26 June 1995 (in German).

constitution permits out-of-area use of German forces and at the political level as to priorities and basic objectives. The controversy was dominated by differences between the governing parties—the Christian Democratic Union (CDU), the Christian Social Union (CSU) and the Free Democratic Party (FDP)—on the one hand, and the Social Democratic Party (SPD) on the other, not least because the votes of the largest opposition party were needed for an amendment to the constitution, for which a two-thirds majority is necessary.

The dispute was further complicated by the fact that the government was creating a *fait accompli* before political agreement had been achieved by declaring all the missions it approved humanitarian, since all major parties had agreed that such missions were covered by the constitution. Since what was disputed was the dividing line between humanitarian and non-humanitarian missions, the opposition suspected the government of using false labelling tactics for the purpose of getting the armed forces and the public accustomed to out-of-area missions. On the other hand, the government could not simply ignore constitutional reservations, since the FDP, which is part of the government coalition and provides the government with its foreign minister, considered an amendment to the constitution to be necessary.[28]

The ruling coalition of CDU/CSU and FDP was therefore unable to agree on a draft bill until January 1993. In this bill they not only advocated involvement of the German armed forces in UN peace-keeping and peace enforcement missions, provided this was approved by a majority in the Bundestag, but also the use of the German military without a UN mandate. The latter provision is subject to the conditions that a case of 'emergency assistance', as defined in Article 51 of the UN Charter, be involved, that the assistance be provided in a multilateral framework and that parliamentary approval be given with a two-thirds majority.[29] As both political camps lacked the necessary

[28] The dispute between the coalition partners about the involvement of German military personnel in AWACS flights over Bosnia led to a strange compromise. The CDU-dominated government retained the German soldiers in the AWACS while the FDP and SPD filed a complaint against the mission with the Federal Constitutional Court. The Court refused to order a withdrawal, but noted that a decision had not yet been made in the main proceedings. In the case of another petition for an interim injunction filed by the SPD against the participation of a German battalion in UNOSOM II, the Court decided that the involvement of the Bundeswehr in out-of-area missions required the prior approval of a majority of the parliament. This ruling, too, was in force until the Court's final decision on the constitutional issue in July 1994.

[29] Deutscher Bundestag, Drucksache 12/4107, 13 Jan. 1993 (in German).

two-thirds majority, the bills languished in the parliamentary committee after their first reading in the Bundestag. Unable to find a compromise, the political parties waited for the ruling of the Federal Constitutional Court.

In the summer of 1992 the SPD had already introduced a bill proposing an amendment to the constitution with the objective of ensuring German involvement in UN peacekeeping activities. Enforcement missions were not permitted under the bill.[30] At a special party conference held in Bonn some months later it was decided, in the light of experiences in Somalia and the former Yugoslavia, that German involvement in peacekeeping operations could include the armed protection of relief convoys and protection zones, provided their defensive, de-escalatory and humanitarian aspects were respected.[31] This position was confirmed at the party conference in November 1993.[32] Some leading Social Democrats attempted to go further in proposing an amendment which would provide for German involvement in collective enforcement actions, on the condition that the UN undergo reform so that it is not just a mandate-granting institution but is also given supreme command and control. This did not receive support in the party.[33]

In the debate at the end of 1994 ton a possible greater German military contribution in Bosnia and Herzegovina he party leader, Rudolf Scharping, stressing the primacy of UNPROFOR's humanitarian mission, claimed that there was no need for such a decision, thus using the same delaying tactics as the Chancellor.[34] A letter from Scharping to members of the parliamentary group of the SPD, in which he stressed that the participation of the Bundeswehr in the event of UN withdrawal from Bosnia and Herzegovina was an alliance obligation, provoked a harsh negative reaction from the SPD's left wing.[35] Six months later, Scharping issued a statement in

[30] Deutscher Bundestag, Drucksache 12/2895, 23 June 1992 (in German).

[31] *Minutes of the Special Party Conference*, Bonn, 16–17 Nov. 1992, p. 413 (in German).

[32] SPD, Parteitag Wiesbaden, 16–19 Nov. 1993: Perspektiven einer neuen Außen- und Sicherheitspolitik [Prospects of a new foreign and security policy], p. 17 (in German).

[33] The SPD parliamentary group submitted a comprehensive motion on UN reform. See Deutscher Bundestag, Drucksache 12/1719, 4 Dec. 1991 (in German).

[34] 'SPD zu Gesprächen über einen deutschen Beitrag bereit' (note 24); and 'Scharping nennt Diskussion über Bosnien hypothetisch' [Scharping calls discussion on Bosnia hypothetical], *Süddeutsche Zeitung*, 4 Jan. 1995 (in German).

[35] Lafontaine, O., deputy leader of the SPD, 'Die neuen Kreuzritter' [The new crusaders], *Der Spiegel*, 2 Jan. 1995, pp. 21–22 (in German); and interview with Heidemarie Wieczorek-Zeul, *Der Spiegel*, 9 Jan. 1995, p. 16 (in German).

the name of the SPD executive board stressing the need to strengthen the security of UNPROFOR by a multilateral force and approving logistical support by the German Bundswehr 'only for a clear UN peacekeeping mission under UN command' while objecting to any mission by German ground forces and combat aircraft.[36] Nevertheless, at least 40 members of the SPD parliamentary group voted in favour of the government decision.[37] Thus, the SPD is still facing tensions within its own ranks on this issue.

As for the other parties in the Bundestag, Alliance 90/the Greens and the former communist Party of Democratic Socialism (PDS) all reject the idea of combat missions under the UN flag. PDS policy would limit the tasks of the German armed forces to national defence, while the Greens, although advocating in their 1994 federal election platform the long-term goal of abolishing both NATO and the Bundeswehr, restrict their conditional support to traditional peace-keeping.[38]

German politicians use a variety of sometimes superficial arguments to back their respective positions, many of which are motivated purely by tactical considerations. The proponents of greater military engagement refer, for example, to the need for Germany to regain full sovereignty and again become a 'normal' state, Germany's growing international responsibility, its image, the expectations of other countries, the future of NATO and the dangers of Germany pursuing a separate foreign policy. Its opponents stress the historical legacy of Germany, the danger of a re-nationalization and re-militarization of German foreign policy, the inefficacy of military means in ensuring peace and the necessity of Germany contributing to a 'civilizing process' by peaceful means.

Although some of these arguments partly make sense, they all miss the crux of the matter. What does it mean to become a normal state? What kind of greater responsibility is to be assumed? Which image should the country work for and for what reasons? When is a separate course dangerous and when is it legitimate? Does not Germany's

---

[36] Presseservice der SPD, Mitteilung an die Presse, 276/95, 12 June 1995 (in German).

[37] Of 655 MPs, 386 approved the decision of the government, 258 were against and 11 abstained. The ruling parties have 341 seats; thus at least 45 MPs of the SPD and the Greens backed the decision of the government. See 'Germans vote to send unit and planes', *International Herald Tribune*, 1–2 July 1995.

[38] Bündnis 90/Die Grünen, *Bundestagswahlprogramm* [Bundestag election programme] (Bornheim, 1994), pp. 6 ff. (in German). See also the interview with the leader of the parliamentary group of the Greens, Joschka Fischer, *Süddeutsche Zeitung*, 3 Jan. 1995 (in German).

difficult historical legacy demand greater German involvement in UN missions? Could not a far-reaching commitment to international institutions like the OSCE or the UN be an effective strategy to prevent the danger of re-nationalization and re-militarization? Is an international civilizing process possible without the option of enforcing the observance of international law? The last question leads to the core of the debate between 'realists' and 'institutionalists'.[39] For realists the national interest and freedom of manœuvre come first. The institutionalists primarily seek collective security within international organizations in order to reduce the danger that the UN will be used for purely national purposes.

VII. The armed forces

The Bundeswehr is undergoing a complicated process of restructuring which will restrict its participation in UN missions for the rest of the 1990s. Since unification Germany has had to tackle three structural problems in relation to its armed forces: (*a*) the merging of two armies; (*b*) the implementation of NATO force structure guidelines following the promulgation in 1991 of the alliance's new Strategic Concept; and (*c*) preparations for out-of-area missions.[40] Since the promulgation of Defence Planning Guidelines for the Bundeswehr in November 1992[41] and the Defence White Book in April 1994,[42] the main tasks of the Bundeswehr are flexible crisis and conflict management in an extended geographical environment, peace missions and humanitarian assistance. These are tasks for which the Bundeswehr is neither trained nor equipped. They require multinational, readily available, highly mobile and flexible components available for deployment in both the whole of the NATO area and globally. Equipment must be adapted and improved and priority given to logistics,

[39] Ehrhart, H.-G., 'Zehn Thesen zur Rolle der UNO in Friedensprozessen' [Ten theses on the role of the UN in peace processes], *Sicherheit und Frieden*, no. 4 (1992), pp. 214–15 (in German).

[40] Correspondingly, the structure of the Bundeswehr is being adapted, and will in future consist of 3 branches: crisis reaction forces, which are immediately available, main defence forces, which are largely dependent upon mobilization, and a basic military organization, which will form the basis of the armed forces.

[41] Bundesministerium der Verteidigung, *Verteidigungspolitische Richtlinien* [Defence policy guidelines] (Bonn, 26 Nov. 1992) (in German).

[42] *Weißbuch 1994* (note 4), p. 41–45.

command, control and communication capacities, transport facilities and intelligence.

Given that each year in the 1990s Germany will have to transfer to the eastern part of the country 150–200 billion DM and that the defence budget is already shrinking, the process of restructuring the Bundeswehr will be very difficult to pursue according to schedule and will leave little room for UN missions.[43] However, the Bundeswehr is continuing to prepare for such operations.[44] In view of the more dangerous environment in which peacekeeping operations are currently being deployed, only military units ready for action will be assigned. Until recently the common assumption was that only light-armoured forces were suited for this kind of mission. Correspondingly two of the five existing light-armoured brigades should become units for UN missions. Bearing in mind the necessity of rotation, Germany will not be capable of making available more than two battalions for the rest of the 1990s.[45]

This goal has meanwhile been replaced by a more flexible but also more obscure approach. The Bundeswehr's crisis reaction forces, which comprise mostly mechanized brigades and whose main task is the defence of Germany and its allies against aggression as well as multilateral crisis management in the framework of NATO or the WEU, are now also supposed to be ready for UN missions. While the air force and the navy already have the military capacity to participate in 'robust' peacekeeping operations, the ground forces' light brigades are as yet only able to be used in traditional peacekeeping. Even such engagements have turned out to be problematic. In the case of

[43] According to the permanent secretary of the German Defence Ministry, Gen. Hans Schönbohm (Retd), the defence budget was reduced by 18% in real terms between 1989 and 1993 and will fall by a further 25% in 1995. See 'Besorgt um deutsche Rüstung' [Worried about German armaments], *Frankfurter Allgemeine Zeitung*, 14 Apr. 1994 (in German).

[44] For example, in 1994 the infantry college of the German Army in Hammelburg also became a centre for UN training. In Jan. 1995 a new command and control centre was established in the Ministry of Defence for commanding German contingents operating abroad under a UN mandate and to enable Germany to become a 'lead nation'. See 'Bonn will Führungsrolle bei UNO-Missionen' [Bonn claims lead role in UN mission], *Die Welt*, 19 Nov. 1994 (in German); Feldmeyer, K., 'Die Schwierige Normalität' [Difficult normality], *Frankfurter Allgemeine Zeitung*, 12 Jan. 1995 (in German); and Bundesministerium der Verteidigung, Ressort konzept zur Anpassung der Streitkräftestrukturen, der Territorialen Wehrverwaltung und der Stationierung [Departmental concept of the adaptation of the structure of the armed forces, the administration of defence and stationing of forces], 15 Mar. 1995, pp. 3 ff. (in German).

[45] Two battalions for UN missions will be established within Airborne Brigade 25 and Ranger Brigade 23. See Albert, B., 'Krisenreaktionskräfte des Heeres' [Crisis reaction forces in the army], *Wehrtechnik*, no. 2 (1994), pp. 6–8 (in German).

Somalia the German battalion had to be formed using soldiers detached from more than 380 offices and units. While they did a commendable job in a very delicate mission and gained valuable experience in operating in an unfamiliar environment, they were also fortunate not to be drawn into a combat situation requiring a high degree of unit cohesion and combat skill.

Because of a lack of political and strategic clarity, the Bundeswehr faces an identity crisis. As Defence Minister Rühe put it, 'Germany is encircled with friends'. This calls into question the legitimacy of Germany's armed forces: for what political purpose will Germany have to maintain what kind of army? The official answer has been that: (a) there are new risks and new tasks; and (b) the 1990 Treaty on the Final Settlement with Respect to Germany stipulates that Germany must reduce its army to 370 000 soldiers by 1995.[46] It is now obvious that the Bundeswehr will be further reduced for budgetary and organizational reasons. Rumours suggest targets from 325 000 to as low as 200 000. In his 1994 report to the Bundestag, the parliamentary commissioner for the armed forces criticized the negative effects of volatile and unsteady plans on the self-confidence and motivation of soldiers.[47] In April 1994 Defence Minister Rühe made public the main conceptual guidelines of his budget cuts which necessitate a reduction of the armed forces to 340 000 and a further reduction of the period of conscription from 12 to 10 months.[48] This provoked a clash with the defence specialists of his own party as well as with the Foreign Minister.[49] In October 1994, the coalition partner of the CDU/CSU revealed new plans from the Defence Ministry indicating a further reduction to 325 000.[50]

The lack of financial resources necessitates new political guidelines since the problems of the German Army are growing. First, there will

[46] For the text, see Vertrag über eine abschliessende Regelung in Bezug auf Deutschland vom 12 Sep. 1990 [Treaty on the Final Settlement with Respect to Germany of 12 Sep. 1990], *Europa-Archiv* no. 19 (1990), pp. 509–14 (in German); or Treaty on the Final Settlement with Respect to Germany, *SIPRI Yearbook 1991: Arms Control and Disarmament* (Oxford University Press: Oxford, 1991), pp. 611–14.

[47] Deutscher Bundestag, Drucksache 12/6950, 8 Mar. 1994 (in German).

[48] The Conceptual Guidelines were published 3 months later. See *BW–aktuell*, 28 July 1994, 2 Aug. 1994 and 4 Aug. 1994 (in German)

[49] The SPD favours a Bundeswehr of 300 000 men. See *Diskussionsentwurf Regierungsprogramm 1994* [Discussion draft of the government programme1994] (Bonn, 1994), p. 32 (in German).

[50] Inacker, M., 'Die FDP stellt Bundeswehr-Umfang und Wehrpflicht-Dauer in Frage' [The FDP calls the size of the Bundeswehr and the length of national service into question], *Welt am Sonntag*, 30 Oct. 1994 (in German).

inevitably be the problem of a two-class army if the shrinking means at the disposal of the Defence Minister are concentrated on the German crisis reaction forces. Second, a further reduction will lead to the problem of inequity in conscription which again provokes the very delicate question of whether or not Germany should maintain a conscript or professional army.[51] The latter would be better suited for out-of-area missions, but it is extremely costly and incompatible with the 'citizen in uniform' ideal which inspires Germany's conscript army and which legitimizes military forces solely for defending the country against an aggressor. The guiding principle is 'being able to fight in order not to be forced to fight'. However, new tasks arising from Germany's new international obligations may require another image oriented according to 'the real conditions of war, danger and human misery'.[52] Hence, the Bundeswehr is torn between old ideals and new tasks in the search for its identity, the outcome of which will have effects on Germany's future military role.

VIII. German society

The debate within German society about the future contribution of Germany to UN crisis management and conflict resolution is to a great extent influenced by the lessons of Germany's belligerent past. One of these lessons is a certain disdain for traditional power politics and the use of military force. Germans have learned to accept the latter only for self-defence and in the framework of a defensive alliance. They have become used to having a minor status in NATO and being protected in return. Hence Germany has become a prosperous and influential civilian power.[53]

As a conscript army the Bundeswehr is part of German society. Consequently it reflects the values, problems and deficiencies of that society, which on the one hand is undergoing a difficult integration process after the formal unification of two separate states and on the

[51] Following the Conceptual Guidelines (see note 48), the 50 000-strong crisis reaction forces will comprise mostly professionals and contracted soldiers. Conscripts can serve in these forces on a voluntary and extended basis for 12–23 months. They are indispensable for the functioning of the crisis reaction forces because they are intended to make up roughly one-third of total strength, but it is not clear if there will be enough volunteers.

[52] *Verteidigungspolitische Richtlinien* (note 41), p. 33.

[53] Ehrhart, H.-G., *The New Germany in a Changing Environment* (Queen's University: Kingston, Ont., 1994); and Maull, H. W., 'Germany and Japan: the new civilian powers', *Foreign Affairs*, vol. 63, no. 5 (winter 1990/91), pp. 91–106.

other is a post-modern civil society characterized by individualism, internationalization and interdependence. Finally German society is democratic, and any kind of international involvement needs the support of the electorate. This is especially true of future military engagements.

Even if the value of public opinion polls is questionable, they give an impression of the general trend of opinion. One significant revelation of German opinion polls is declining comprehension of the future tasks of the Bundeswehr. The younger generation especially is less imbued with a sense of military service. The percentage of conscientious objectors has risen steadily from 14 per cent in 1988 to 30 per cent in 1993.[54] Doubts seem to be growing, moreover, in society as a whole. The proportion of those who think that the defence budget ought to be further reduced has grown steadily from 12 per cent in 1978 to 65 per cent in 1992.[55] While the need for national defence is not called into question by over 90 per cent of the population, polls indicate at least five other interesting trends. First, attitudes on Germany's future international role are shifting from a reserved stance toward greater approval of a more active role (from 48 per cent in 1990 to 62 per cent in 1992).[56] Second, it does not follow from this that there is support for greater military involvement of the Bundeswehr abroad. While participation in traditional UN peacekeeping or humanitarian assistance missions is usually approved of by more than 50 per cent and 90 per cent respectively, support for enforcement actions is only 12–26 per cent.[57] A poll within the Bundeswehr shows that 68 per cent of draftees (89 per cent of professionals) are in favour of German participation in peacekeeping operations in Europe, 56 per cent approve of peacekeeping operations outside Europe (79 per cent of professionals) and 57 per cent approve of German participation in

[54] Deutscher Bundestag (note 47), pp. 18–20.

[55] Hoffmann, H.-V., *Demoskopisches Meinungsbild in Deutschland zur Sicherheits- und Verteidigungspolitik 1992* [Opinion poll in Germany on security and defence policy] (Akademie der Bundeswehr für Information und Kommunikation: Waldbröl, 1993), p. 29 (in German).

[56] Wulf, D., Deutschland im Wandel: Ergebnisse einer repräsentativen Studie [Germany in change: results of a representative survey] (unpublished, 1993. In German).

[57] SPD Bundestagsfraktion, Presse-Mitteilung 1090, 7 May 1993 (in German), in which 4 polls conducted by different institutes between Dec. 1992 and Apr. 1993 are compared. In a poll conducted after the Muslim defeat in Bihac, 36% were in favour of sending German jet fighters to Bosnia, while 54% were against. See *Die Woche*, 9 Dec. 1994. This result was confirmed 6 months later, when 55% of Germans polled opposed sending Tornados to Bosnia. See 'Bonn bites the Balkan bullet but still ducks Bosnia', *International Herald Tribune*, 27 June 1995.

UN military activities.[58] Third, there is far greater resistance in the eastern part of Germany to any kind of international military engagement. Fourth, political setbacks to the dispatch of some types of German contributions to peacekeeping missions indicate that there is not yet a stable consensus on Germany's role in this kind of international engagement.[59] Fifth, Germans expect a lot of the UN. For 94 per cent the main task of the UN is the establishment of a worldwide peaceful order. While 51 per cent think that national armed forces should be substituted by the UN in the long run, 41 per cent are in favour of the UN seeking a monopoly on the use of military force.[60]

IX. Facing the peacekeeping challenge

On the one hand, Germany is assuming a greater role in the UN, as is evidenced by its election to the UN Security Council for 1995–96 and by the appointment of two Germans as top UN officials.[61] On the other hand, the support of the German Government for UN peacekeeping seems not to be without its limits; hence, for intance, its negative response to the UN Secretary-General's request for a German stand-by peacekeeping contingent.[62] Public reaction in Germany to the events in Somalia indicated rapidly declining public support for an incoherent UN mission. In principle Germany could participate

[58] Hoffmann (note 55), pp. 232 ff. Unfortunately the terms 'peacekeeping operations' and 'UN military activities' are not specified.

[59] For example, during the Persian Gulf War support for participation of the Bundeswehr in peacekeeping operations dropped to 24%. At the beginning of 1993 a similar decline was measured. See Hoffmann, O., *Deutsche Blauhelme bei UN-Missionen* [German blue helmets on UN missions] (MVG-Verlag: Munich 1993), pp. 77–79 (in German).

[60] Hecker, G., 'Im Aufwind' [On the up], *Information für die Truppe*, no. 4 (1994), pp. 16–17 (in German).

[61] Gen. Manfred Eisele has been appointed Assistant Secretary-General heading the Office of Planning and Support in the Department of Peace-keeping Operations. The diplomat Karl-Theodor Paschke has been appointed UN Inspector-General.

[62] A major political dispute erupted between the Foreign Ministry, which approved German stand-by forces, and the Defence Ministry, which objected and—with the backing of Chancellor Helmut Kohl—finally won. See 'Heftiger Kampf um Einsatzliste' [Fierce quarrel over standby list], *Süddeutsche Zeitung*, 16 Jan. 1995 (in German); 'Bundesregierung verweigert Ghali konkrete Zusagen' [Federal government refuses Ghali concrete commitments], *Süddeutsche Zeitung*, 19 Jan. 1995; and 'Butros Ghali wirbt für Einsatztruppe' [Boutros-Ghali canvassing for reaction force], *Süddeutsche Zeitung*, 20 Jan. 1995 (in German). The Defence Minister's reported reluctance to provide any support for the UN resulted from a cabinet resolution of summer 1993 stipulating that all costs of German missions abroad must be paid from the Defence Ministry budget, which had already been deeply cut. See Förster, M. and Knopfdruck, P., 'Internationale Blamage?' [International shame?], *Behörden-Spiegel*, Feb. 1995, p. 10 (in German).

today in all kinds of UN activity. However, it still has to go through a long learning process. While peacekeeping operations have a reasonably good chance of gaining wide acceptance, this will be jeopardized by confusing them with enforcement actions, which may result in military escalation. This is not to say that military enforcement should necessarily be opposed, but that its terms and tasks have to be as clear as possible.[63] However, no matter whether the UN or the OSCE is involved, the main goal for international relations that is acceptable in a democratic society such as Germany's is the gradual construction of a comprehensive collective security system which permits a transition from the law of the strongest to the strength of law. This should be the standard of Germany's international engagement, providing both a goal consistent with its basic values and a yardstick for decisions about whether or not to become involved in armed conflicts.

[63] Ehrhart, H.-G. and Klingenburg, K., 'Was ist Peacekeeping?' [What is peacekeeping?], *Hamburger Informationen zur Friedensforschung und Sicherheitspolitik*, no. 15 (1994) (in German).

3. Japan

Takao Takahara

I. Introduction

The Japanese are the quintessential newcomers to UN peacekeeping. The deployment of 27 civilians to Namibia in October 1989 as part of UNTAG was the first instance of participation by Japan. In February 1990, although it was not officially classified by the UN as a peacekeeping operation, six civilians joined ONUVEN, which oversaw the Nicaraguan elections. In both these cases those sent were exclusively civilians. The dispatch of Japanese military personnel was at that time unthinkable, mainly because of constitutional constraints.

In September 1992, under a new law (Law on Cooperation in UN Peacekeeping and Other Operations) which had been enacted in August after bitter controversy, some 600 troops of the Japanese Self-Defense Forces (SDF) were deployed to Cambodia as part of the Military Component of UNTAC. In addition 41 Japanese civilians joined the Electoral Component and 75 police officers were attached to the Civilian Police Component. Participation in UNTAC has so far been the largest and most widely publicized instance of Japanese involvement in UN peacekeeping. In September 1992 three civilians took part in UNAVEM II. After May 1993, 53 SDF personnel also participated in ONUMOZ, 48 of them in Movement Control and 5 as staff officers of the Military Component. In March 1994, 15 Japanese civilians joined the electoral division of ONUSAL to oversee the elections in El Salvador. From October to November 1994, 15 Japanese civilians supported the work of ONUMOZ during the Mozambican elections.

What has been controversial on all these occasions is the dispatch overseas of personnel of the Japanese military. Japan's unwillingness to use its military force in international peace operations has been criticized as a cowardly reluctance to endanger the lives of its citizens. This reluctance must be understood in its historical and constitutional context.

II. Constitutional and historical restraints

In Japan, as in Germany, the question of military participation in international peacekeeping arouses domestic debate concerning the constitutionality of such action. The relevant clauses of the Japanese Constitution of 1947 are its Preamble and Article 9.[1]

At first sight these clauses appear to disarm Japan totally, as was explained by the government at the introduction of the draft constitution to the Diet in 1946. A majority of constitutional scholars in Japan—around 80 per cent—also subscribe to the view that Article 9 prohibits the maintenance by Japan of any significant military force.[2] Accordingly, there are strong doubts about the very constitutionality of Japan's military forces. The issue has caused one of the most significant rifts between the progressive opposition parties and the governing Conservatives in post-war Japanese politics.

The 'pacifist clauses' of the constitution are so sweeping that they might seem to have been imposed on the Japanese against their will. In 1947 when the new democratic constitution was enacted, Japan was totally disarmed and still under the occupation of Allied forces following World War II. The key to understanding the situation is to distinguish the general public's attitude from government policy. While the government was generally lukewarm about the imposed constitutional reform, the general public welcomed and strongly supported the new constitution, including the pacifist clauses. Opinion polls taken in May 1946 showed 85 per cent of respondents supporting the draft constitution, with 70 per cent believing that Article 9 was necessary and only 2 per cent thinking otherwise.[3] Since then roughly 70 per cent have consistently shown support for the pacifist clauses.

To the government and a large proportion of politicians, total demilitarization was an anomaly which should be corrected in due course. As cold war confrontation became the dominant framework of international politics, the remilitarization of Japan as a bulwark against communism became a goal of the USA. This change logically should have brought about abolition of Article 9. In the 1950s the ruling Conservatives actually tried to revise the constitution, mainly in order to make rearmament legal. However, popular support for the

---

[1] Both are reproduced in appendix 3A of this chapter.
[2] Norimoto-Tsuneoka, S. *et al.*, *The Constitution of Japan* (Kashiwa Shobo: Tokyo, 1993), p. 140.
[3] Norimoto-Tsuneoka (note 2), p, 6.

'Peace Constitution' was impossible to override. In a series of elections the Conservatives failed to gain the required two-thirds majority in the Diet, where leftist opposition parties represented the popular voice on this issue. According to opinion polls, even if the revisionist Conservatives had overridden the opposition in the Diet it seemed unlikely that the amendment would have been supported by a simple majority in the referendum that was required to follow.

The reasons behind public opposition to revision of the constitution are twofold. First, the attempt to revise the constitution was seen as a reactionary move by the old politicians to erode the political and social reforms achieved under the years of occupation. Revisionists of the constitution also argued for restriction of basic rights by emphasizing the duties of citizens and restoration of the status of the Emperor, whose role was depoliticized by the constitution. In the political struggles in post-war Japan, retaining the constitution thus also meant adhering to the newly installed post-war democracy.

Second, the pacifism symbolized in those clauses meant more to the impoverished post-war generation than just the disarmament imposed by the occupation forces. It was seen as a precious lesson from the experience of the devastation of modern total war, helping to ensure that Japan would never tread that path again. The image of a New Japan, reborn from the ashes to be a peaceful, non-militarist nation, became a matter of national identity for a significant proportion of the post-war Japanese. This allergy towards anything with a 'smell of gunpowder' is strengthened by occasional glimpses of the remnants of militarism in Japanese society.

There is a third factor which has worked as an obstacle to the revision of the pacifist constitution. For the Allies, one of the major reasons for disarming the Japanese and for stationing the US military on Japanese soil was to placate the fears of neighbouring countries by corking the spectre of Japanese militarism in the pacifist bottle once and for all. Protests from Asian nations which experienced Japanese occupation could not be overlooked by the revisionists (however insensitive they have otherwise been). There was therefore a tacit alliance between concerned Asian neighbours and the Japanese people against the revival of Japanese militarism. All these factors played a significant part in the debate over the dispatch of SDF personnel to the UN peacekeeping operation in Cambodia in 1992–93.

Unlike Germany, post-war Japan did not achieve a constitutional consensus on rearmament; until recently the leftist opposition parties held to their basic stand that the SDF were unconstitutional. The revisionists were confronted with the reality that amendment of the pacifist clauses was impossible. Reconciliation of the constitution with another reality, ongoing Japanese rearmament, was made by reinterpretation of these clauses, namely to read Article 9 as meaning that Japan is allowed to maintain armed forces so long as they are strictly limited to self-defence. Starting with the premise that the right of self-defence is not forsworn by the first paragraph of Article 9, successive governments have read the second paragraph as implying that the maintenance of certain forces for self-defence is permitted. Hence the name Self-Defense Forces and the fact that the SDF lack certain characteristics of normal military forces.[4] The government also explains that the constitution limits the right of self-defence to 'individual self-defence', meaning that the right of 'collective self-defence' stipulated in Article 51 of the UN Charter is restricted under the present constitution. For this reason the US–Japanese military arrangements are legally constructed not so much as an alliance but rather as a base leasing arrangement.[5]

Under this reinterpretation of Article 9 the accumulation of constitutional *faits accomplis* has continued to the present, creating a military force with a budget matching those of the world's major military powers. Efforts to establish legal consistency have been made by the bureaucracy. Appeals to the traditional legal interpretation of Article 9 have been the tactic of the opposition in their efforts to mobilize public concern over the incremental enlargement of the sphere of constitutionality.[6] Reflecting public concern, the SDF impose certain restrictions on themselves with respect to equipment and activities.[7] They have on the whole kept a low profile and been careful not to appear to resemble the Imperial Army or Navy of the pre-war militar-

[4] For example, it has no military court.

[5] The US–Japanese 1954 Mutual Defence Assistance Agreement and the 1960 Treaty of Mutual Co-operation and Security have been explained to the Japanese not as a part of regional security system in the Western Pacific but as a guarantee by the USA to protect Japan in the case of an attack in return for providing military bases.

[6] For a succinct description of the role of legal norms in the issue of Japanese remilitarization, see Katzenstein, P. J. and Okawara, N., *Japan's National Security: Structures, Norms and Policy Responses in a Changing World* (Cornell University East Asia Program: Ithaca, N.Y., 1993), pp. 118–37.

[7] For example, long-range bombers and aircraft-carriers are perceived to exceed the limits of self-defence.

ist Japan. In winning public support, the SDF's commitment to disaster relief has proved to be one of its most successful efforts, to the extent that many Japanese see the SDF as useful primarily for disaster relief and only secondarily for the defence of the country. Thus the SDF have never been involved in military action; not a single person has been the casualty of military action by the SDF since their establishment.

Opinion polls show that the majority of the public have accepted the existence of the SDF, especially since the 1970s. However, support has been passive and conditional on the benign character of the SDF. At the end of the cold war no political force was ready to take the initiative to revisit the issue in response to the radically changed international environment. The whole issue of military participation in UN peacekeeping thus remains a challenge to the old frame of reference— the 'peace issue' or 'rearmament issue' of the cold war days—and demands from the Japanese a huge learning exercise. In this context the Cambodian experience was a true milestone.

III. The Cambodian experience

As early as 1946 the Imperial Diet, when debating the pacifist clauses of the draft constitution, took up the question of Japan taking part in UN forces. With Japan under occupation and not yet a member of the new international organization, the question was dismissed as unrealistic. Later the official government position was that as long as a UN operation did not involve the use of force the constitution did not prohibit the SDF from participating. However, since the existing legislation on the SDF did not stipulate such participation, it is understood that at present the SDF could not participate in these activities.[8]

The dispatch of SDF personnel to UNTAC, their first overseas deployment, was made possible by new legislation, the Law on Cooperation in UN Peacekeeping and Other Operations (called the 'PKO bill' in the Japanese media). This legislation was the outcome of a long and bitter controversy which followed the submission of the bill to the Diet in September 1991. It passed the Diet in June 1992, overcoming fierce opposition from the two leftist opposition parties. The public was divided over this issue. A poll conducted just before the passage of the law indicated that 41.6 per cent of respondents

[8] Official position expressed by the Japanese Cabinet, 28 Oct. 1980.

favoured SDF participation in UN peacekeeping, while 36.9 per cent were against. When asked about the constitutionality of the dispatch, 50.3 per cent thought that it was problematic while 28.2 per cent thought otherwise.[9]

In order to gain support for the bill from the centrist opposition parties, the government accepted several binding restrictions. This was also necessary to respond to a certain scepticism within branches of the government such as the Cabinet Legislation Bureau. In accordance with the traditional notion of UN peacekeeping, the 1992 law restricts Japanese participation in peacekeeping to cases where agreement on a cease-fire among conflicting parties exists and the neutrality of UN forces is sustained. In addition, states surrounding the host state must all accept Japanese participation. The law also stipulates that once these conditions cease to exist, the Japanese must be promptly withdrawn.

Other compromises included 'freezing' SDF participation in certain common peacekeeping activities, such as monitoring the cessation of armed conflict or demobilization of armed forces, stationing and patrol in buffer zones, inspecting the movement of arms, collecting abandoned weapons and assisting exchange of prisoners of war—until further legislative action is taken.

The reason for such restrictions is the question of the constitutionality of the use of armed force by the SDF: whether, in the case of an attack by hostile groups, organized use of force by the SDF to defend themselves would constitute a violation of the pacifist clauses of the constitution. The judgement of the Cabinet Legislation Bureau was that it would be. In their view organized military action which involves use of arms is constitutional only for the defence of Japan, and a peacekeeping mission could not be counted as such.

The 600 SDF personnel dispatched to Cambodia did not therefore participate in the Military Component of UNTAC as an infantry battalion, but joined as engineers and repaired roads and bridges. The participation of the SDF as an organization in UNTAC's military observer group was also interpreted as illegal: eight Japanese officers who joined the military observer group went as individuals, formally separated from the engineering battalion.

Efforts were thus made to limit the SDF's activities to missions where the use of arms seemed unlikely. However, what would have

[9] Asahi Shimbun, 12 June 1992.

happened if the SDF had been attacked? The law stipulates that troops may only bear 'small-sized weapons'. Accordingly in Cambodia they were equipped with pistols and rifles which were to be used only in cases where the life and security of the individual soldier were endangered. The government also explained that the SDF would not be placed under the operational command of UNTAC, meaning that they would retain the right to independent command and could not be forced into military action.

These restrictions were later criticized as being remote from realities in the field. Disciplined, organized action with regard to the use of arms was precisely what was required in order to keep hostilities in Cambodia to a minimum. During the debate over the PKO bill, the government tried to evade the problem by contending that the SDF would only be sent to situations where violent incidents were unlikely.

This was the background to the reported excessive concern of the Japanese in Cambodia about their own safety. Apparently Japan's wish to keep the SDF in a relatively safe district was heeded and in September 1992 the engineering battalion established its camp in the relatively calm province of Takeo to the south of Phnom Penh.

Playing down the inherent dangers of the Cambodia operation, as the government appeared to have done in order to soothe sceptics during the Diet debates, resulted in a severe backlash when actual casualties occurred. A Japanese UN Volunteer was killed with a Cambodian interpreter in April 1993 in the more dangerous province of Kompong Thom. Early in May a group of Japanese civilian police officers was attacked in the north-western province of Banteay Meanchey. One police officer was killed and four others injured. These incidents aroused much emotion in Japan.

Even without these incidents, as the Cambodian election in May 1993 approached and one of the parties to the Paris Peace Accords, the Khmer Rouge, withdrew its cooperation, the possibility of withdrawal from UNTAC was raised publicly in Japan. One of the conditions of Japanese participation—accord between all parties in the region—seemed to have eroded. This point was also raised within the government, especially after the Japanese fatality in May.

The government was in a difficult position. It was criticized for not listening to earlier warnings from Japanese personnel in Cambodia that the situation was quite different from the way it was explained before they left Japan. In particular the police allocated to the UNTAC Police Component had problems. They had been told that their mission was to supervise and control the local police force and were unprepared to actually police a region where local police did not exist. Unlike the SDF they were stationed in the more unstable regions where they faced problems caused by the withdrawal of the Khmer Rouge from the peace process. One of their lodgings was attacked by rockets and burned as early as January 1993, fortunately in their absence.

To many in Japan it seemed as if the government was deliberately deceiving the public in order to evade straightforward debate on the constitutional question. Sympathy focused on the two Japanese killed, who were viewed not only as having sacrificed their lives to the cause of bringing peace to Cambodia but also as being victims of government mismanagement or, as some saw it, dishonesty. The criticism was all the stronger because it reminded people of the practices of the former Imperial Army and Navy, which paid little regard to the lives of their personnel. Some commentators warned of the danger of making the victims heroes who were faithful to their duties to the state.

The government, forced to take action, requested UNTAC to relocate the Japanese police to safer areas, but this self-interested plea was necessarily rejected by UNTAC. Japan did not decide to withdraw, however, and a team of civilians was sent soon after the second incident in May to join the Electoral Component of UNTAC to assist in the polling process. The number of team members was reduced from 53 to 41 after the Japanese deaths.

The tragic incidents in Cambodia did have an educational effect on the Japanese public. The victims were not SDF personnel, and this fact drew more attention to the non-military aspect of peacekeeping. In the heated debates over the dispatch of the SDF, the whole picture of the UNTAC mission, which included important civilian elements such as the Human Rights and Repatriation Components, had been under-reported. The effect on the younger generation of this more balanced account of UNTAC's role was encouraging, as shown for example in the increase in the number of applicants for places among the Japan Overseas Cooperation Volunteers.[10] An initiative of

---

[10] Japan Overseas Cooperation Volunteers (JOCV) is a Japanese version of the Peace Corps. About 1000 persons accepted twice a year. The number of applicants used to fluctuate

Mr Takehito Nakata, the father of the dead UN Volunteer, to establish a fund for UN Volunteers was also warmly received.

This refocusing on the non-military aspects of peacekeeping resonated with the thinking already prevalent among the Japanese people. The question 'Does it really have to be the SDF?' had been often raised. While recognizing a need to participate in UNTAC, people had been wondering whether it was in fact by sending the military that Japan could contribute best. Such doubts were strengthened as news reports showed the engineering battalion in action rebuilding roads and bridges. If the place is safe, some argued, why send the SDF instead of construction workers?

Although many questions raised during the debates stemmed from ignorance of UNTAC and of requirements in the field, their basic orientation was fairly clear. An opinion poll conducted immediately after the passage of the 1992 law on peacekeeping was indicative. To the question 'How should Japan contribute to international society?', respondents were asked to choose as many as they liked from a list of options. The top choice was 'by providing personnel for disaster relief and helping refugees' (60.4 per cent). Then came 'efforts to preserve the global environment' (59.2 per cent) followed by 'economic assistance to other countries' (43.4 per cent). Well down the list appeared 'participation in peacekeeping operations' (23.9 per cent), with 'political leadership' (18.5 per cent) falling behind that.[11] The results reflect the 'honourable allergy'[12] of the Japanese public towards the military and use of force. On the other hand, the non-military image of the SDF mission in Cambodia worked positively towards acceptance of its use overseas. Television images of the SDF engineer battalion coincided with that of the familiar SDF at work in disaster relief. In the same vein, an amendment of the International Relief Force Bill, which now included the SDF as participants in any Japanese relief force to be dispatched overseas at the request of affected countries, was introduced at the same time as the PKO bill and encountered relatively few objections.

Overexposure of the SDF in news reports on Japanese participation in UNTAC did, however, reflect public concern over the constitutional issue. The handling of the issue by the government streng-

around 3500 each time, but increased until in Nov. 1994 it exceeded 6300, more than half of them women.

[11] *Yomiuri Shimbun*, 28 June 1992.

[12] *New York Times* editorial, 2 June 1992.

thened the impression that the priority was to make the use of the SDF overseas a *fait accompli*. This was understandable in the context of the post-war struggle over the rearmament issue.

One argument used by sceptics in their campaign against the deployment of the SDF overseas was Japan's neighbours' fear of a possible resurgence of Japanese militarism. The notorious reluctance of the Japanese Government to make reparations to the victims of war crimes was referred to in the same vein, as the sceptics questioned whether Japan was morally qualified to send its military overseas. In a sense the 'apologies' expressed by successive cabinets after the fall of the conservative Liberal Democrats in August 1993 could be seen as a cynical tactic to ease the dispatch of the Japanese military abroad.

The difficulty that opponents of SDF deployment had was in coming up with a clear alternative. Non-military assistance was discussed but no concrete political initiative taken to launch a creative new project along those lines. The SDF, on the other hand, had behaved well during their mission, persevering under the critical gaze of many Japanese journalists. Their discipline was also apparently satisfactory. Thanks to the success of UNTAC, the SDF personnel returned from Cambodia to a warm welcome in September 1993.

IV. Prospects

The issue of military participation in peacekeeping was one of the major issues in Japan during 1992 and the summer of 1993. The introduction and passage of the much-debated PKO bill, the dispatch of the SDF to Cambodia and Mozambique, and the deaths of the UN Volunteer and civilian police officer all received ample press coverage. Since the Cambodia operation ended, however, the issue has attracted less public attention; headlines have been devoted to the political revolution shaking Japan. Press coverage of the return of SDF troops from the successful operation in Mozambique in January 1995 was minimal. This does not mean that the problems have disappeared.

First, the ongoing political turmoil is itself closely related to the issue of the constitutionality of the SDF. The totally incompatible attitudes of the Conservatives and the Progressives on the constitutionality of the SDF has impeded positive change in government for decades. The Social Democratic Party of Japan, which had long been the champion of constitutional pacifism, decided to shelve the issue in August 1993, which made it possible to form a coalition government under Morihiro Hosokawa. It did, however, sustain its minimalist attitude towards the dispatch of the SDF to participate in UN peace-keeping, while conservative parties in the Hosokawa coalition took more activist positions on this issue. This was the background to the government's reluctance to dispatch troops to Macedonia in January 1994. The Macedonian case was problematic, being a preventive deployment, a type not mentioned explicitly in the PKO bill, and the situation seemed too unpredictable to judge whether it would meet the bill's other conditions. If pursued, the Macedonian deployment issue could have destabilized the frail coalition in the midst of a struggle in the Diet over electoral reform.

The Social Democrats took a big step in July 1994 when Tomiichi Murayama, their chairman and Prime Minister, declared the SDF constitutional under certain conditions, overriding protests from the pacifist wing of the party. On 20 July Murayama stated in the plenary session of the lower house that he believed that the SDF, so long as they limit their actions strictly to self-defence and use the minimum force required, could be recognized as constitutional.

After some hesitation, in August Murayama also dispatched the SDF to Zaire to take part in the Rwandan refugee relief operation from September to December. This was in response to a request from the UN High Commissioner for Refugees (a Japanese, Mrs Sadako Ogata) and was not part of the UN peacekeeping mission in Rwanda. The 'humanitarian international relief operations' clause of the PKO bill was applied for the first time. Among some 260 ground troops sent to Camp Goma in Zaire, just under half were professionals in relief activities such as doctors and sanitary workers; others were there to guard and maintain facilities for the SDF personnel. In addition, 118 air personnel, most of whom were stationed in Nairobi, took part in transport duties and assistance for international relief activities. There was great scepticism about the relevance and effectiveness of sending the SDF to a refugee camp for just three months. There were also anxieties over whether SDF personnel might be put in a situation where the single machine-gun which they brought with them had to be used. Fortunately, no serious incident occurred.

In November 1994, Murayama's coalition government passed an amendment to the SDF legislation to enable the overseas dispatch of

SDF transport planes for the purpose of airlifting Japanese nationals when their lives are threatened in a local conflict. These ground-breaking steps were taken partly in an effort to sustain the peculiar coalition between the prime adversaries of the cold war days, the Socialists and the Liberal Democrats. At the time of writing it is uncertain how voters will react to these developments. With the public still divided over the constitutionality of the SDF and its activities, however, the issue can be expected to remain one of the major factors dividing the political forces in the course of Japan's continuing political transformation.

Second, in mid-1995 there was a review of the controversial peace-keeping law, as stipulated in the legislation. The foremost issue was whether or not to 'unfreeze' the restricted activities of the SDF. Some politicians indicated their preference for this step.[13] Although they were a small minority, other prominent politicians argued for a new construction on the constitutional question, beginning with the premise that any SDF force dispatched should be placed completely under UN command. Hence the use of force would not be an act of the Japanese state and would not violate the constitution, making it logical to unfreeze the restraints on the SDF's peacekeeping activities. The majority of politicians were at that stage cautious about unfreezing, reflecting the continuing split in public opinion.[14]

Third, the Defense Agency has started a reassessment of the National Defense Program Outline of 1976, which has served as the doctrine for Japanese defence policy. This will probably result in a reorientation and restructuring of the SDF, including a revised policy towards peacekeeping. At present, participation in UN peacekeeping is only a side-job for the SDF. Some believe it could become the best rationale for retaining the SDF after the cold war, although the recent focus on North Korea's nuclear capabilities might give new life to the SDF's traditional self-defence role. It was expected that major points

[13] For example, the Chief Secretary of the centrist Komeito (Clean Government Party) announced this idea as early as in Mar. 1993. See *Asahi Shimbun*, 29 Mar. 1993.

[14] A poll conducted among some 300 government officials indicated that 24% believed that the restraints should be removed immediately, while 25% were for retaining them. The majority, 46%, thought that they should be removed at some time in the future but that now was not the time to do so. See *Asahi Shimbun*, 3 Apr. 1994. According to another opinion poll, only 13% were for immediate removal, 48% thought that restrictions should remain for a few more years and 23% were against any future removal of such restraints. See *Yomiuri Shimbun*, 9 June 1994.

of the overall review would be formalized by late 1995 in order to be reflected in the 1996 budget.[15]

Fourth, in a longer-term perspective, a consistent posture on peacekeeping will have to be determined if Japan is to seek new security arrangements in its region. Since the end of the cold war, moves have gradually begun to establish comprehensive regional security forums in the Asia–Pacific region such as ARF (the ASEAN Regional Forum).[16] Giving new meaning to the current US–Japanese security arrangements is also on the agenda. Peacekeeping would provide possible areas of regional cooperation, such as joint training or establishing facilities for such training. For the SDF, peacekeeping could become a way of joining in regional military cooperation while continuing to refrain from participating in collective self-defence arrangements.

Finally, the issue is also seen to be linked with the quest of Japan for a permanent seat on the UN Security Council. Foreign Ministry officials are known to be particularly keen on this, nor do the public dislike an idea which generates national pride. There is, however, significant scepticism among the public as to whether Japan really is ready to assume the necessary obligations. Besides a need to increase its diplomatic capacity (the Japanese diplomatic corps is relatively small compared with those of Western nations), concern is focused on the possibility of Japan being required to fulfil military obligations as peace operations become increasingly important in the work of the Security Council.

Although reassurance has been given by the UN Secretary-General that permanent membership of the Council does not necessarily entail military duties, political voices within some of the present permanent member states, including elements in the US Senate, have explicitly called on Japan to assume military obligations if it is to become a permanent member. For some politicians who would like Japan to become a 'normal state', this accords with their agenda: international obligations will pressure Japan to relinquish its post-war pacifism. But will the Japanese public agree to scrap the long-held symbol of a reborn pacific Japan?

[15] *Yomiuri Shimbun*, 31 Dec. 1994.
[16] ASEAN is composed of Brunei Darussalam, Indonesia, Malaysia, the Philippines, Singapore, Thailand and Viet Nam. The ARF includes the 7 ASEAN states plus Australia, Canada, China, the European Union (EU), Japan, South Korea, Laos, New Zealand, Papua New Guinea, Russia and the USA.

The popularity among the Japanese of the idea of Japan becoming a permanent member of the Security Council is strongly linked with the view that this would not be achieved on the basis of Japan's military might (the self-declared non-nuclear status of Japan being symbolic in that respect). It would show nations seeking military prowess that there can be different paths to attaining an honoured place in international society. Relatively low support in Japan for acquiring permanent membership compared with the levels of support in other candidate countries seems to reflect anxieties on the part of the Japanese public about being forced into military involvement.[17]

On UN peacekeeping itself, the public is still split over SDF participation. According to an opinion poll taken in March 1994, those who believe that the participation of the SDF in UN peacekeeping is constitutionally problematic constituted 44.8 per cent of the total, while 45.8 per cent answered otherwise. The former group had declined from 55.9 per cent when the same question was asked in June 1992 at the time of the passage of the 1992 peacekeeping law, while the latter group had grown from 34 per cent at that time.[18] Although there is general approval of the Cambodian experience, it is restrained.[19]

The puzzle is not yet solved. On the one hand, strong sentiment is evident among the public towards Japan remaining a strictly civilian power. Aversion to anything military and scepticism about the true motives of the government when it enthusiastically promotes military matters are both ingrained in the psyche of many post-war Japanese as a lesson learned the hard way by their parents and grandparents.[20] On the other hand, there is broad agreement on the desirability of Japan

[17] While 55% of American, 62% of British and 73% of German respondents believe that Japan and Germany should become permanent members of the Security Council, 51% of Japanese respondents agree with the idea. See *Asahi Shimbun*, 2 Apr. 1994. Another opinion poll conducted by the Foreign Ministry showed that 53% of respondents were for permanent membership, 32% did not know and only 15% were against. However, of those who responded positively, 39% were against any military involvement including in peacekeeping operations. See *Asahi Shimbun*, 5 June 1994.

[18] *Yomiuri Shimbun*, 31 Mar. 1994.

[19] Polls taken after the successful elections in Cambodia show restrained approval of SDF participation in UNTAC, with remaining scepticism. When asked whether the dispatch of troops was good or not, 46% answered affirmatively and 33% negatively. See *Asahi Shimbun*, 2 June 1993. Given a choice among 4 alternatives, namely 'strongly approve', 'somewhat approve', 'somewhat disapprove' and 'totally disapprove' of SDF participation, one poll showed the respective figures of 14.2%, 47.9%, 27.4% and 8.0%. See *Nihon Keizai Shimbun*, 16 June 1993. Another poll with the same options showed 14.9%, 40.6%, 31.8% and 8.1%, respectively. See *Yomiuri Shimbun*, 3 July 1993.

[20] In contrast to the situation in some other countries, it is unthinkable for a political leader in Japan to gain public support by propounding the use of force overseas.

contributing to international peace efforts, not only by providing financial help but also by human participation. This would be in total accord with the principles stated in the Preamble of the constitution.

If Japan is to commit itself to international cooperative efforts, the commitment should be stable and credible. In order to keep the commitment credible, stable public support is essential. The Japanese Government is still struggling to win public confidence on this issue. It will have to convince the people both that it is different from the post-war constitutional revisionists, who were atavistic nationalists, and that it is not hiding something from them. It will also have to convince Japan's neighbours of the peaceful intentions of Japan. From the perspective of the people this will mean strengthening democratic control over security issues, along with significant arms reduction and the devising of creative non-military ways to contribute to international efforts towards peace. New political initiatives to fill such gaps are yet to come.

Appendix 3A. The 'pacifist clauses' of the Constitution of Japan

Preamble

We, the Japanese people, acting through our duly elected representatives in the National Diet, determined that we shall secure for ourselves and our posterity the fruits of peaceful cooperation with all nations and the blessings of liberty throughout this land, and resolved that never again shall we be visited with the horrors of war through the action of government, do proclaim that sovereign power resides with the people and do firmly establish this Constitution. Government is a sacred trust of the people, the authority of which is derived from the people, the powers of which are exercised by the representatives of the people, and the benefits of which are enjoyed by the people. This is a universal principle of mankind upon which this Constitution is founded. We reject and revoke all constitutions, laws, ordinances, and rescripts in conflict herewith.

We, the Japanese people, desire peace for all time and are deeply conscious of the high ideals controlling human relationship, and we have determined to preserve our security and existence, trusting in the justice and faith of the peace-loving peoples of the world. We desire to occupy an honored place in an international society striving for the preservation of peace, and the banishment of tyranny and slavery, oppression and intolerance for all time from the earth. We recognize that all peoples of the world have the right to live in peace, free from fear and want.

We believe that no nation is responsible to itself alone, but that laws of political morality are universal; and that obedience to such laws is incumbent upon all nations who would sustain their own sovereignty and justify their sovereign relationship with other nations.

We, the Japanese people, pledge our national honor to accomplish these high ideals and purposes with all our resources.

. . .

Article 9

Aspiring sincerely to an international peace based on justice and order, the Japanese people forever renounce war as a sovereign right of the nation and the threat or use of force as means of settling international disputes.

In order to accomplish the aim of the preceding paragraph, land, sea, and air forces, as well as other war potential, will never be maintained. The right of belligerency of the state will not be recognized.

4. Russia

Dmitriy Trenin

I. Introduction

The collapse of the rigid communist system and the resulting disintegration of the Soviet Union have revealed enormous potential for conflict in an area formerly known for its strict totalitarian discipline. Under Stalin, the main architect of the multinational Soviet state, of the 160 or so ethnic groups which had their homeland in Central Eurasia 54 received varying degrees of largely nominal, but in all cases territorially based, autonomy. This preference for territorial over cultural autonomy had dramatic consequences. Between 1985 (the beginning of *perestroika*) and 1993, some 60 conflicts erupted between ethnic groups, of which 32 led to violence and 8 degenerated into what could be described as wars.[1] They were mainly wars over territory. Casualties (killed and missing) numbered 800 in 1991 but over 50 000 in 1992 in Tajikistan alone.[2] The refugee population in 1992 has been conservatively estimated at 1.5 million in the Transcaucasus and about half that number in Tajikistan. There have been no wars so far between the Soviet successor states (although Armenia and Azerbaijan have come close) and not everywhere have the emerging tensions spiralled out of control. There was no inter-ethnic violence in 35 national–territorial units; 9 other areas were successfully 'pacified' before 1989.[3] Contrary to what most Soviets, including the political élite, believed until the mid-1980s, the 'nationalities issue' had been merely frozen rather than resolved by communism.

In the wake of the disintegration of the Soviet Union a vast security vacuum appeared. Instability spread. Of all the successor states, only the Russian Federation was capable, in principle, of acting to preserve or restore peace within the former Soviet Union. From late 1991 to early 1992, however, the Russian leadership was more interested in withdrawing from the burdensome Soviet empire than in pacifying its

[1] Alaev, E., *Rossiyskaya Gazeta*, 16 July 1993 (in Russian).
[2] Payin, E. (member of the Presidential Council), 'Mozhet li Rossiya byt mirotvortsem?' [Can Russia become a peacekeeper?], *Izvestia*, 29 Sep. 1993 (in Russian).
[3] *Rossiyskaya Gazeta*, 28 Aug. 1993. National–territorial units are those subjects of the Russian Federation with an ethnic reference, such as Tatarstan and Chechnya. There are in total 89 subjects of the Federation.

troublesome parts. Disengagement remained the main theme. Russian troops left Nagorno-Karabakh in early 1992 and even before that had evacuated South Ossetia in Georgia. They were ordered to take a passive role in the rest of Georgia and in Tajikistan, which were fast becoming ungovernable, and to cut short an operation against Chechen separatists in the northern Caucasus almost before it began. Ethnic conflicts were viewed by the authorities and by the general public not as an invitation for urgent action, such as some form of peacekeeping, but rather as a compelling reason to 'bring the boys home'.

Russia had had very limited previous experience with peace-keeping. Although Soviet military observers served in UNTSO in Egypt and Syria as early as 1973, there were only a few dozen of them, all officers. Their presence was largely symbolic and had no impact on Soviet military thinking. It was only in 1991 that Soviet/Russian participation in UN peacekeeping was broadened to include observers on the Iraq–Kuwait border, in Western Sahara, Cambodia and Mozambique, and for the first time in 1992 ground troops in the former Yugoslavia. Hence, as Russian military officers admitted, in establishing a peacekeeping capability for the former Soviet Union they had to proceed very much by trial and error.[4]

The development of a conceptual framework followed, rather than preceded, Russian peacekeeping operations. Flight from the 'imperial legacy' was quickly rejected as impractical. Unlike the classical European empires, the Soviet Union's territory was contiguous with its conquests. Borders between the Russian metropolitan area and the periphery were non-existent or blurred. Redeploying divisions and whole armies to Russia from these territories while the withdrawal of Soviet forces from Central and Eastern Europe was still incomplete proved difficult or impossible. Some Russian garrisons, suddenly in the middle of a war zone, became isolated fortresses, their arms depots often ransacked and individual soldiers rendered targets for local warring factions. In many cases, the ethnic Russian population and other groups in the areas of conflict looked to the Russian Army as their only protector. Left without precise instructions and disoriented, some commanders started to act on their own. It was in these circumstances that more active Russian intervention finally occurred.

---

[4] See, for instance, *Krasnaya Zvezda*, 12 May 1993 (in Russian).

There are four distinct kinds of operation currently lumped together under the name 'Russian peacekeeping':

1. *Traditional peacekeeping.* This follows a cease-fire agreement and involves cease-fire monitoring. It is successful in military terms if disengagement is achieved, hostilities are stopped and further bloodshed is prevented. Political stalemate puts the whole attempt at conflict settlement in jeopardy. Examples are South Ossetia and the Trans-Dniester region.

2. *Peace enforcement or low-intensity conflict.* Here there is no cease-fire agreement and hostilities continue, with Russian forces supporting one side against the other. There is a danger of Russia being dragged into conflicts from which it will have difficulty in extricating itself. Tajikistan is a clear example.

3. *Uncoordinated actions by Russian forces which find themselves in a war zone.* Abkhazia and Tajikistan before late 1992 are examples.

4. *Internal peacekeeping.* Military operations are carried out in the territory of the Russian Federation during a state of emergency. North Ossetia/Ingushetia is an example.

The first kind of operation is open to international cooperation. The more cooperation, the better, not least for Russia. The second kind should be examined most closely. At a minimum, they should be recognized as something very different from traditional peacekeeping either on the UN or on the Russian models. The third should not be permitted to assume an independent dynamic. The fourth requires a most careful national strategy, for the future of the Russian Federation may be at stake.

Characteristically, Russia has preferred to talk and act in terms of 'creating', that is restoring or imposing, peace rather than simply keeping it. The Russian word *mirotvorchestvo* means, literally, peace creation. Russian political parlance does not distinguish between peacekeeping and peacemaking; the exact Russian equivalent of peacekeeping is an unwieldy phrase very rarely used. The drafters of the bill on peace operations in the Russian Parliament found it difficult to define what a peacekeeping operation is and how it differs from operations to restore or enforce peace.[5] This absence of a legal

---

[5] This chapter follows SIPRI usage and employs the term 'peacekeeping' except where operations to restore or enforce peace are clearly meant. On the bill, which became law in June 1995, see section II below.

definition allowed General Yevgeniy Podkolzin, Commander of the Russian Airborne Forces, to refer to the Chechnya operation begun in late 1994 as 'peacemaking'.

There has always been more to Russian peacekeeping than restoring order where chaos was threatening or preventing the spread of violence once it had broken out. Stopping bloodshed and protecting human lives were put into a broader context. The concept of national interest, gradually accepted during 1992–93 by the bulk of the Russian political class, proceeded from the central premise of Russia's continued great-power status or *derzhava*.

Raw geopolitics was thus rediscovered after years of an official 'class approach' and a brief interlude of preaching 'universal human values'. As a dominant power in Eurasia and the largest successor state of the Soviet Union, Russia was proclaimed to have vital interests and 'special rights' in the former Soviet republics. It became commonplace to refer to the 'unique geopolitical/geo-strategic space' of the former Soviet Union or to the 'near abroad'. Russia's positions there, in the official view, were not to be abandoned.[6]

A domino theory (Tajikistan destabilizing Uzbekistan and splitting Kazakhstan and, finally, taking Islamic fundamentalism to the banks of the Volga River) became accepted wisdom in Russian Government circles. Destabilization in the Russian northern Caucasus was feared if the Russian Federation withdrew from the Transcaucasus, with the ensuing chaos likely to be exploited by the neighbouring regional powers, both of them Russia's traditional rivals. Thus, despite the formal separation of the republics, Russia was finding it increasingly difficult to stay aloof from developments within its new neighbouring states—because, the government said, of its multifaceted links with them—while protesting at the same time that its involvement should not be viewed as an attempt to exclude the newly independent states from the sphere of international relations.[7]

Most Russian statesmen see no other way of building stability than active Russian diplomatic, economic and military involvement. It seems clear to them that conflicts, inevitable as part of the nation-building process, 'make necessary the presence and participation of Russian military peacekeeping contingents for preventing and over-

[6] Interview with Foreign Minister Kozyrev, *Izvestia*, 8 Oct. 1993 (in Russian).

[7] Kozyrev, A., 'Rossiya fakticheski v odinochku nesyot bremya realnogo mirotvorchestva v konfliktakh po perimetru svoikh granits' [Russia is carrying the burdens of peacekeeping in conflicts on its borders alone], *Nezavisimaya Gazeta*, 22 Sep. 1993 (in Russian).

coming crisis situations'.[8] Claims for a 'special Russian role in the post-Soviet space' are matched by a sense of responsibility as the successor state of both the Tsarist Empire and the communist Soviet Union.[9] To this Russian diplomacy would add a kind of *mission civilisatrice*—upholding the values of the OSCE, including those relating to minority rights.[10]

Restoring a measure of stability along the periphery of the new Russian borders (which with the exception of those with the Baltic states are mostly borders in name only) has become a major security problem. As every student of Russian history knows, the absence of 'natural' borders has always been a salient factor of Russian history, driving territorial expansion 'for strategic reasons'. With the western approaches perceived, after the end of the cold war, as being relatively secure, and the Far Eastern frontier unchanged, it is the southern border, from the Caucasus to the Caspian Sea to the steppes of the southern Urals and southern Siberia, which has become the main concern. Full transparency of borders with the war-torn Caucasus and Central Asia has aggravated the inevitable spillover effect (weapon proliferation, the spread of crime, terrorism and epidemics), but closing the borders would cost more than Russia could afford.[11]

Increasingly it is the approximately 25 million ethnic Russians and 4 million other people with roots in the Russian Federation, including such 'divided groups' as the Ossets (in Russia and Georgia) and the Lezgins (in Russia and Azerbaijan), which are cited as a powerful reason for Russian involvement. The 90 000-strong Russian community suffered heavily during the conflict in Abkhazia; roughly half of the once 300 000-strong ethnic Russian population of Tajikistan has fled the horrors of civil war.

Altogether, the dissolution of the Soviet Union left some 70 million people outside their republics of origin. Many of these are returning to the 'metropolitan republic', Russia. In 1992–93 the Russian Federa-

---

[8] Kharchenko, D. K. (Lt-Gen.), 'The experience of the Russian armed forces in peace-keeping operations in the areas of local conflicts', Report presented to the Military Committee of the 39th General Assembly of the Atlantic Treaty Association, Athens, 30 Sep. 1993, p. 2.

[9] Piskunov, A. (member of the State Duma), 'Rossiya i mirotvorchestvo: Doklad na seminare Severoatlanticheskoy Assamblei "Teoriya i praktika podderzhaniya mira"' [Russia and peacekeeping: Report to the Seminar of the North Atlantic Assembly on Theory and Practice in Peacekeeping], London, 23 Feb. 1994, p. 2 (in Russian).

[10] Kozyrev, A., *Nezavisimaya Gazeta*, 27 Oct. 1993 (in Russian).

[11] Some estimates put the price of constructing 1 km of a new border at *c.* $60 million.

tion became home to some 2 million displaced persons from the former Soviet Union, a heavy financial burden. Between 3 and 6 million more ethnic Russians are expected to arrive in Russia from the other republics of the former Soviet Union in 1995–98. Housing conditions and the employment situation in Russia are extremely poor and continue to deteriorate. The government, lacking financial and other resources, would much prefer to keep these 'other Russians' or 'ex-fellow Soviets' in their current places of residence. It knows that, if too many immigrants arrive in the Russian Federation at the same time, the situation may explode, paving the way, some liberals fear, for an 'overtly nationalistic dictatorship and, through it, to a Yugoslav scenario'.[12] The Chechen crisis of 1994–95 made that scenario appear more likely.

This legitimate concern is sometimes presented as warranting a continued Russian military presence in the newly independent states. The issue of Russian troop withdrawal from the Baltic states has thus been repeatedly linked, in particular by the military, to Russian minority rights. Russia has also long insisted on acceptable guarantees for the Russian-populated Trans-Dniester region of Moldova as a precondition for the withdrawal of the Russian 14th Army. One of the most powerful arguments for keeping Russian troops in Tajikistan has been the need to protect the 180 000-strong Slav community there from the danger of a resumed civil war.

No matter how 'artificial' former Soviet administrative boundaries may appear now that they have been upgraded to international borders, Russia has another important stake in preventing forcible border changes, whether in Azerbaijan, Georgia or Moldova: the unity of the Federation will be called into question unless this cardinal principle is upheld and reasonable limits are placed on the principle of self-determination of nations. Armed conflicts within the Russian Federation are considered almost as dangerous to national security as local wars just outside Russia's borders because they threaten Russia's vital interests and 'could be used as a pretext for interference in her internal affairs by other states'.[13] The territorial conflict between the North

---

[12] Kozyrev, A., 'Russia's peacemaking: there are no easy solutions', *New Times International*, no. 4 (1994), pp. 16–18 (in Russian).

[13] 'Osnovnye polozheniya voennoy doktriny Rossiyskoy Federatsii' [Basic provisions of the military doctrine of the Russian Federation], *Krasnaya Zvezda*, 19 Nov. 1993, p. 11 (in Russian). A translation into English appeared in *Jane's Intelligence Review*, Special Report, Jan. 1994.

Ossetians and the Ingush in the northern Caucasus, which broke out in October 1992, was the first major armed confrontation inside Russia. The operation in Chechnya, begun in December 1994, turned into the most intense armed conflict in the former Soviet Union since 1991.

Peacekeeping is a major foreign affairs topic on the national political agenda. The range of views is extremely wide, from advocacy of a 'clean withdrawal' to promotion of peacekeeping as a vehicle of imperial restoration. So far, withdrawal has proved impossible. In 1992 and 1993 Russian policy in the territory of the former Soviet Union, including its peacekeeping aspect, was being shaped against the background of the power struggle in Moscow between the ruling moderate reformers and the opposition national patriots. While the former were represented in the government, the latter formed a majority bloc in the then Supreme Soviet. Paradoxically, but only superficially so, those openly supporting the restoration of the Soviet Union looked for allies among the arch-separatists (for example, in the Trans-Dniester region and in Abkhazia) who were undermining the newly independent successor states from within. Since each party in the Russian capital possessed its own instruments of power until the October showdown in 1993, Russia was in fact pursuing two conflicting policy lines *vis-à-vis* the Caucasus and Moldova, which was clearly destroying Russia's credibility as a peacekeeper.

Since the December 1993 parliamentary elections the State Duma, the lower house of parliament, has been on the whole supportive of the idea of peacekeeping, but has insisted on more legislative control over its conduct. Russian peacekeeping is opposed by some liberals, who believe that it is too challenging a mission for demoralized Russian troops, and by the ultra-nationalist Liberal Democrats (the party of Vladimir Zhirinovsky) who consider Russian soldiers 'too good to have their lives wasted in somebody else's wars'.

Public opinion is not particularly favourable to Russian peacekeeping operations. A poll conducted in the autumn of 1993 showed that only 17 per cent of respondents supported the use of Russian troops to stop conflicts; 27 per cent agreed, but only on condition that it be done for the protection of ethnic Russians; 49 per cent were against any employment of troops; and 7 per cent were undecided. A uniform pattern was observed in all age and social groups. The professional military personnel polled were guided by a desire to help stop conflicts, rather than by any 'patriotism', while managers showed almost the opposite attitude. The intelligentsia were against any involvement, while the managerial élite were most favourably disposed towards it.[14]

II. The legal and policy framework

Russian officials insist that Russian peacekeeping is firmly based on the relevant provisions of international law, the UN Charter (especially Chapters VI, VII and VIII) and the 1992 Helsinki Document.[15] Also cited are the various multilateral agreements signed within the CIS at its 1992 Kiev and Tashkent summit meetings (on the status, recruitment procedures and deployment patterns of military observers and collective peacekeeping forces) and various bilateral agreements.

Because no public law on peacekeeping existed in Russia until June 1995, for several years peacekeeping operations had no status in Russian law. The 1992 Law on Defence[16] declared the repulsion of external aggression to be the only mission of the Russian armed forces. The bill on 'the procedure for provision of military and civilian personnel of the Russian Federation for participation in operations to maintain or restore international peace and security and other peacekeeping activities' was only approved by the Federal Assembly and signed into law in June 1995.[17] The new law only provides a general framework for the provision of personnel for such operations.

The new Russian military doctrine, adopted in November 1993,[18] lists 'actual and potential hotbeds of local wars and armed conflicts, above all in direct proximity to Russian borders' among the more serious sources of military threat to Russia. The list also includes 'suppression of the rights, liberties and lawful interests of the citizens of the Russian Federation in foreign states' and 'attacks against military facilities of the Armed Forces of the Russian Federation deployed in the territory of foreign states'—both very likely occurrences during

---

[14] *Segodnya*, 14 Sep. 1993 (in Russian).

[15] CSCE, Helsinki Document 1992: The Challenges of Change (CSCE: Helsinki, 1992). Excerpts from the Helsinki Document were published in *SIPRI Yearbook 1993: World Armaments and Disarmament* (Oxford University Press: Oxford, 1993), pp. 190–209.

[16] The text of the law was published in *Rossiyskaya Gazeta*, 9 Oct. 1992 (in Russian).

[17] Federalny zakon o poryadke predostavleniya Rossiyskoy Federatsiey voennogo i grazhdanskogo personala dlya ychastiya v deyatelnosti po podderzhaniyu ili vosstanovleniyu mezhdunarodnogo mira i bezopasnosti, *Sobranie Zakonodatelstva Rossiyskoy Federatsii*, no. 26 (26 June 1995).

[18] 'Osnovnye polozheniya voennoy doktriny Rossiyskoy Federatsii' (note 13), pp. 5.

such conflicts. The same doctrine authorizes the use of armed forces for 'internal' peacekeeping, as in Chechnya.

The military doctrine places emphasis on local wars and conflicts in which Russian forces might take part. At the same time it explicitly provides for participation in peacekeeping operations ordered by the UN Security Council or carried out 'pursuant to Russia's international commitments'. Sometimes, as the example of Tajikistan appears to show, the difference between the two is blurred. The CIS High Command, which first developed a general military approach to peacekeeping, envisaged a peacekeeping force as one of two main components of future joint armed forces.[19] Another confusing element is the indiscriminate use of the term peacekeeping with regard to troop activities based on no international agreement (as, for example, in Abkhazia in 1992–93).

Consent of all parties and perceived impartiality are the essential requirements for peacekeeping as traditionally understood by the United Nations. Russian officials insist that the Russian Federation acts 'in all cases with the consent and at the request of the parties to the conflict'.[20] This is true of Moldova and South Ossetia but certainly not of Tajikistan, where the Russian-led CIS peacekeepers have the invitation of the government in Dushanbe, but not of the opposition.

When involved in peacekeeping activities, the mission of Russian forces, in theory, is to separate the conflicting sides, protect humanitarian aid convoys and evacuate the civilian population; they should also isolate the area of conflict to ensure the effectiveness of any international sanctions that may have been applied to the parties.

In practice, while in South Ossetia and Moldova Russian peacekeepers arrived following cease-fire agreements, of which Russia was a guarantor, in Tajikistan no such agreement has so far been reached. Despite agreements concluded within the CIS, other Commonwealth countries have been reluctant to join the Russian Federation as partners in keeping the peace. Russia has had to act unilaterally, but in the most unorthodox way: units of the conflicting sides take part in peacekeeping operations alongside the Russians. A joint staff, composed of the adversaries and the Russians, is the main operational authority. Even observation posts, patrol parties and picket teams

---

[19] Burutin, G. (Col-Gen.), *Rossiyskaya Gazeta*, 20 Aug. 1993 (in Russian).
[20] Kozyrev (note 7).

often have a mixed composition.[21] The same formula had been envisaged for Nagorno-Karabakh[22] before it was agreed at the CSCE summit meeting in Budapest in December 1994 that the CSCE rather than Russia would be responsible for keeping the peace there. Russian contingents are the dominant element of the joint peacekeeping forces, sometimes being several times more numerous and always much better equipped than those of the other participants. In South Ossetia for several months in 1992–93 the Russians were the only active element of the joint peacekeeping force because the Georgian and Ossetian sides were unable to keep their battalions on duty through the winter.

In internal armed conflicts federal forces are usually expected to be deployed before, not after, a cease-fire agreement has been reached. In theory, once a state of emergency has been declared and after they arrive in the conflict area, Russian forces should physically disengage the warring sides and create a demilitarized zone. This is considered to be a job for the military: internal security forces are said to be unable to separate the conflicting sides. Inside the demilitarized zone each battalion, company and platoon is assigned its area of responsibility. They proceed to impose and monitor a cease-fire, disarm illegal armed formations, help enforce law and order, and carry out mine-clearing. The case of Chechnya demonstrates, however, that what might originally be conceived as a police action could, under certain conditions, degenerate into full-scale war.

III. The management of peacekeeping

Training and planning for peacekeeping

It is widely believed in Russia that peacekeeping is essentially a military undertaking. Consequently only good soldiers are thought to make good peacekeepers. Basic military training with an emphasis on command, control, communications and intelligence (C^3I) is thus considered essential, as are an ability to act independently and exercise initiative, special psychological training and an awareness of legal issues. The key training exercises include separation of warring parties, monitoring and patrolling, search and detention of transgres-

---

[21] For example, in Moldova 13 out of 41 posts are jointly manned by Russian and Moldovan or Russian and Trans-Dniestrian troops. See *Izvestia*, 5 Apr. 1994 (in Russian).

[22] *Krasnaya Zvezda*, 2 Mar. 1994 (in Russian).

sors and, if need be, 'liquidation of bandit formations'.[23] Legal issues such as the use of weapons, rules for detention and search of civilians, and some basic elements of criminal law are also included in the curriculum.

The only training base for Russian peacekeepers at present is the training centre of the 27th Motorized Rifle Division (MRD) of the Volga Military District (MD) at Totskoye, in the Orenburg region. The training lasts at least six months, of which some three and a half are devoted exclusively to peacekeeping. Since the leading academies or war colleges in Russia have shown little interest, the MD tasked with peacekeeping has had to initiate its own training programme. Officers have had to 'learn on the job'.[24] Suggestions have been made that a special department should be opened at the Frunze Academy or at the Vystrel Higher Officers Courses.

The army's first peacekeeping field training exercise, held in March 1994 in Tajikistan, provides some idea of the reality of Russian peacekeeping. During the exercise the troops were told to stop the enemy's advance by using artillery and airpower and then to counter-attack and defeat him. Guns and mortars, multiple-launch rocket systems, helicopters, ground-attack aircraft and fighter aircraft were used.

Configuration of forces and deployment patterns

Russian peacekeeping forces were created at the end of 1991 as part of the Armed Forces of the Russian Federation.[25] A proposal to attach a standing Peacekeeping Force to the Ministry for Emergency Situations was rejected for the time being. Russian military observers were posted on the Armenia–Azerbaijan border in 1991 and along the Gumista River in Abkhazia in 1993, in both cases to very limited effect. In contrast, Russia's troop contingents in South Ossetia (one battalion) and in Trans-Dniester (initially four battalions, now two) have been successively keeping the peace since mid-1992. In Tajikistan, a large unit, the 201st MRD, has been involved since 1992, together with Russian border troops and forces from several Central

[23] *Krasnaya Zvezda*, 12 May 1993 (in Russian).

[24] *Krasnaya Zvezda*, 12 May 1993 (note 23).

[25] Interview with Major-Gen. Anatoliy Sidyakin, CO, Division of Peacekeeping Forces, *Krasnaya Zvezda*, 12 May 1993 (in Russian).

Asian states, in a low-intensity conflict officially referred to as a 'peacemaking' operation.

By mid-1992 some 15 000 soldiers were involved in various peace operations. Nine battalions were successively deployed to South Ossetia and the Trans-Dniester region. This necessitated upgrading regular military units to 'peacekeepers', at least formally. Although Russia still has a military force of just under 2 million,[26] which it is unable to reduce quickly, there is a considerable shortage of officers and men for peacekeeping. It is envisaged that in future one or two army divisions (15 000–16 000 troops) will be designated as peacekeeping forces. The 27th MRD may then be joined by the 45th MRD (Leningrad MD). Ironically, Russia still has troops deployed throughout all the conflict areas of the former Soviet Union except Nagorno-Karabakh, but they often cannot be used because of poor discipline.

There is also a general understanding that, in future, peacekeeping operations should be civilian–military in nature, involving civilian personnel, civil police, observers and experts. There is a perceived need for civilian control over such operations. Placing Russian peacekeepers under the Ministry for Emergency Situations (to which, at present, some 100 000 soldiers in civil defence units report) is still a possibility. The ministry's forces have had some experience of humanitarian aid missions in Abkhazia in 1993 and Georgia in early 1994. Any structural change of this kind will, however, require enormous organizational effort.

At present the 27th MRD includes both 'peacekeeping forces units' and 'normal' units (tanks, self-propelled artillery and air defence). In the field, the basic unit is a reinforced infantry battalion. Since not all units of the peacekeeping forces are at full strength, they often have to be reinforced before being deployed to conflict zones.

Recruitment of peacekeepers has seen some changes. Initially most private soldiers were conscripts. Sometimes these 18-year-olds were sent to a conflict zone immediately after basic military training. This was dangerous and ineffective and aroused popular indignation. Conscripts were later replaced by contracted volunteers. Hopes were high, but reports are so far mixed. The number of volunteers is insufficient and their quality uneven. On the other hand the soldiers complain that their remuneration in conflict zones is not commensurate

---

[26] Total numbers were 1 917 400, as of 1 Jan. 1995. Defence Minister Pavel Grachev, quoted by *Krasnaya Zvezda*, 23 June 1995, p. 1 (in Russian).

with the risks. Continued deprivations lead to demoralization. With rotation normally every six months, the resources of the armed forces are stretched thin. As for equipment, Russian peacekeepers have some 800 AIFVs (armoured infantry fighting vehicles), 200 artillery pieces and 187 tanks, totalling over 1300 vehicles.[27]

Decision making

In the absence of a law on peacekeeping, the mechanism for taking decisions and executing them depended on the specific situation. In South Ossetia, the Trans-Dniester region and Abkhazia operations were preceded by top-level agreements signed by the president. The decision on Tajikistan was the product of internal Moscow decision making, with CIS approval being of symbolic value. In this particular instance, as in the case of Chechnya, there are parallels with the way decisions on Afghanistan were made during the Soviet era.

Since the demise of the Soviet Union the top echelon of the Russian Government has been notorious for constant infighting and occasional crises. Under these conditions coordinating national security strategy, including its peacekeeping aspect, has become hostage to the internal political struggle. Allegations by the president's political friends and opponents alike about the paralysis of decision making regarding peacekeeping are numerous.[28]

The 1993 constitution, which abolished the system of Soviets, in theory bolsters the president's role as the principal maker of foreign and defence policy. The new law on peacekeeping, however, sought to define the responsibilities of the executive and the legislature in the area of peacekeeping and prevent the military from becoming a scapegoat for the failures of the national leadership. Previously in the event of Russian participation in UN peacekeeping operations a treaty had to be signed between the Russian Federation and the UN, subject to ratification by the parliament.[29] The Council of the Federation, the upper house of the parliament, thereafter decides on the provision of troops and numbers.[30] The *ex post facto* approval by the Council of

[27] Piskunov (note 9), p. 1.

[28] See Payin (note 2); and Rutskoy, A., *Rossiyskaya Gazeta*, 23 June 1993 (in Russian).

[29] Russia is currently participating in MINURSO, UNAMIR, UNIKOM, UNOMIG, UNPROFOR and UNTSO.

[30] *Krasnaya Zvezda*, 25 Mar. 1994 (in Russian).

the 1994 Abkhazia operation serves as an illustration of how things may proceed in practice.

Within the Foreign Ministry and the Ministry of Defence (MOD) special groups have been established under deputy ministers to deal with matters pertaining to peacekeeping. In addition, the Ministry for Emergency Situations deals with humanitarian assistance. In 1992–93 the Foreign Ministry and the MOD took different, sometimes opposing positions on particular conflicts, for instance in relation to Abkhazia in September 1993. In an attempt to improve interaction within the executive branch an inter-agency commission on peacekeeping was created under the aegis of the Russian Security Council.

Once an agreement between the warring sides has been reached, mixed commissions are to be established which include representatives of the parties to the conflict and Russia. Their mission is to elaborate peace agreements and mechanisms for their implementation. The commissioners not only negotiate but also, in effect, administer the area where a peace operation is being carried out.

Command and control and rules of engagement

Russian peacekeeping forces are normally under the command of a deputy defence minister. Peacekeepers in Tajikistan are, however, officially part of a coalition force whose Russian commander (a three-star general) theoretically reports to the heads of state of Kazakhstan, Kyrgyzstan, Russia and Uzbekistan, who created the force. The chain of command follows the usual Russian Army pattern.

While 'regular' Russian peacekeepers are reasonably disciplined, other Russian forces deployed in conflict areas have had problems.[31] Individual commanders, like General Alexander Lebed of the 14th Army, were allowed to act with unprecedented freedom. In other cases Russian generals were accused of taking orders from leaders of warring parties (such as the late Sangak Safarov in Tajikistan). In still others (for example Abkhazia), a dangerous gap appeared between official military policy (neutrality) and apparent secret instructions to help one of the sides. In their September 1993 offensive the Abkhaz used the AIFVs and artillery pieces which had been placed in the

---

[31] 'Helsinki Watch—rossiyskim vlastyam' [A letter from the Executive Director of Helsinki Watch to the President of the Russian Federation], *Nezavisimaya Gazeta*, 9 Nov. 1993, p. 5 (in Russian).

custody of Russian units in Abkhazia. Some members of the Russian military had presumably concluded profitable deals, including arms and ammunition transfers. Consequently, proposals were made to replace the whole Russian military contingent in Abkhazia. There have been persistent reports, officially denied, about illicit or covert Russian arms supplies to the warring parties in the Transcaucasus.

Whatever rules of engagement are devised, there is one serious psychological obstacle. As Foreign Minister Andrey Kozyrev once put it, 'For some, participation in a peacekeeping operation is still tantamount to combat action on enemy territory from the recent past'.[32] Defence Minister General Pavel Grachev publicly stated that his task in Tajikistan was to take measures 'to control the enemy and defeat him'.[33] Major-General Sidyakin of the 27th MRD refers to the 'internal function' of the peacekeeping forces in the Trans-Dniester region and in South Ossetia.[34] There is talk of a 'war environment', with peacekeepers compared to an 'assault party separated from the bulk of friendly forces'. Professionalism, however, is steadily growing, replacing traditional standards and reducing improvisation.

While there is general understanding that Russia 'cannot withdraw its peacekeeping forces yet' from the areas of tension,[35] there is no desire to keep Russian peacekeepers in the field indefinitely, if only for budgetary reasons. Peacekeeping is currently financed from the defence budget, which displeases the military.

IV. Russian peacekeeping and the international community

While Russian statesmen insist that Russia is 'fated' to play the role of a stabilizing force in the former Soviet Union, especially where Russian interests are affected, the West is suspicious of an emerging 'Monroeski doctrine'. Russia's new assertiveness is interpreted as a sign that it 'seeks, as it did in centuries past, to insure its security by asserting influence over its near neighbours to the west and south'.[36] Peacekeeping by Russian troops has therefore come under close scrutiny. It is feared that such operations, by a country which is

[32] Kozyrev, quoted by *Segodnya*, 6 July 1993 (in Russian).
[33] Helsinki Watch (note 31).
[34] *Krasnaya Zvezda*, 12 May 1993 (note 23).
[35] Col-Gen. G. Kondratev, quoted by *Izvestia*, 5 Apr. 1994 (in Russian).
[36] Whitney, C., *New York Times*, 31 Oct. 1993, p. 5.

clearly not disinterested, could lead to political domination. The hard fact, however, is that until now no other state or international organization has appeared willing to replace or capable of replacing Russia as a peacekeeping force in the former Soviet territories.[37]

Russia would like its special role to be recognized. President Boris Yeltsin said on 28 February 1993 that the 'time has come when authoritative international organizations, including the UN, should grant Russia special powers as the guarantor of peace and stability in the territory of the former Soviet Union'. Whatever reservations the West might have were to be dealt with by drawing on the 'natural reserve of mutual trust among democratic states'. This meant Russia showing understanding of US actions against Iraq and expecting the same from the West *vis-à-vis* Russia's problems in Tajikistan.[38]

In concrete terms, Russia wants its peacekeeping sanctified and financed by the UN. The UN Secretary-General made a counter-proposal in late 1993 that Russian troops should engage in peace-keeping in Asia and the Americas, while peacekeepers from Asia and the Americas were sent to parts of the former Soviet Union. This was immediately called unrealistic by Russia. In the spring of 1994 UN officials let it be known that they might consider sponsoring a peace-keeping operation inside the former Soviet Union provided Russian troops did not make up more than 20–30 per cent of the force.[39] Russia is sincere when it says that it wishes to enlist the support of others, but everything does not depend on them.

Besides political support, Russia also wants burden-sharing. It is heavily engaged in peacekeeping in the CIS, while having to pay a substantial share of expenses for UN peacekeeping operations else-where. The CIS itself is of little help: its other members do not send troops or contribute financially to Russia's efforts despite invitations and their commitments under the Tashkent Protocol of 16 July 1992.[40] Financial support from the UN and the OSCE has thus been requested since early 1993 in the name of the new partnership with the West. The idea of creating a voluntary fund has also been floated. Another possible solution would be to count Russian expenses for peace-

---

[37] In Abkhazia, for instance, the UN initially authorized sending 8–10 observers, and later 80, but only 22 arrived for duty and were still there in early Mar. 1994.

[38] Kozyrev, A., *Segodnya*, 6 July 1993 (in Russian).

[39] *Izvestia*, 5 Apr. 1994 (in Russian).

[40] Sharp, J. M. O., 'Conventional arms control in Europe', *SIPRI Yearbook 1993* (note 15), p. 603.

keeping within the CIS against its contribution to the UN peace-keeping budget.

Initially very hostile to any foreign military presence in the space of the former Soviet Union, Russia's military would now actually welcome genuinely impartial forces, mandated by the UN and/or the OSCE, along the Tajik–Afghan border and in the Transcaucasus. The prospects of that happening remain bleak. In this situation, Russia's most realistic options lie with the CIS, perhaps by turning it into the kind of regional organization mentioned in the UN Charter, like the Organization of African Unity (OAU) or the Organization of American States (OAS), which could be charged with regional peacekeeping. A CIS–OSCE link is also proposed, but the recent record suggests that this will not be easy. Although in September 1992, pursuant to the Sochi Agreement of 24 June 1992,[41] Belarus, Georgia, Kazakhstan, Russia and Ukraine were to have deployed observers to the Armenian–Azerbaijan border, only Russia did so. In Tajikistan the Central Asian military presence is largely symbolic. Thus, Russia is likely to continue its mission single-handedly, without much help, but with external criticism.

V. Conclusion

Russia's peacekeeping record within the territory of the former Soviet Union is mixed. To counter criticism officials in Moscow point out that even the UN 'technology of peacekeeping' remains 'rather imperfect'.[42] Classic peacekeeping was a response to a challenge of a particular time and is now inadequate. Russian peacekeeping, it is claimed, is fully consistent with the UN Charter and does not require approval by any outside body once the conflicting sides have agreed to it. Russian successes in Moldova and South Ossetia, and more recently in Abkhazia, are sometimes contrasted with UN problems in Somalia and elsewhere. On the other hand, Russian actions in Chechnya have damaged the credibility of Russian peacekeeping everywhere. Chechnya, of course, is in a category of its own. It serves as a warning that 'peacemaking' which is ill-conceived, badly prepared and badly executed might be indistinguishable from war.

[41] Reported by Radio Free Europe/Radio Liberty, *RFE/RL Research Report*, 9 Oct. 1992, p. 68.
[42] Kozyrev (note 12), p. 17.

5. The United States

*Donald C. F. Daniel**

I. Introduction

On 3 May 1994, President Bill Clinton signed Presidential Decision Directive (PDD) 25. It laid out his 'Administration's Policy on Reforming Multilateral Peace Operations', defined as encompassing activities from traditional peacekeeping to enforcement. The Directive was the product of 'an inter-agency review of our nation's peacekeeping policies and programs in order to develop a comprehensive policy framework suited to the realities of the post-Cold War period'.[1] The document is unusual for its detail on the criteria which the US executive branch is to apply when making decisions whether and how to support United Nations peacekeeping missions.

This chapter presents some of its main provisions, but it will help the reader's understanding of PDD 25 if the domestic factors which determined its content are presented first. The document was in gestation over a period of a year. During that time several predictions that it was about to be issued proved premature: it was either 'put on hold' or redrafted as the administration contended with deep-rooted and competing foreign policy tendencies, a general US ambivalence towards the UN, the low priority accorded foreign policy in the Clinton White House, the impact of Congress and the related impact of public opinion.[2]

---

[1] US Department of State, *The Clinton Administration's Policy on Reforming Multilateral Peace Operations*, Department of State Publication 10161 (Department of State, Bureau of International Organization Affairs: Washington, DC, May 1994), p. ES1.

[2] Gellman, B., 'Wider UN police role supported', *Washington Post*, 5 Aug. 1993, p. A1; Holmes, S., 'Clinton may let US troops serve under UN chiefs', *New York Times*, 18 Aug. 1993, p. A1; Sciolino, E., 'US narrows terms for its peacekeepers', *New York Times*, 23 Sep. 1993, p. A8; Lewis, P., 'US plans policy on peacekeeping', *New York Times*, 18 Nov. 1993, p. A7; and Schmitt, E., 'US set to limit role of military in peacekeeping', *New York Times*, 29 Jan. 1994, p. A1. The quotation is from Gordon, M. and Friedman, T. L., 'Disastrous US raid in Somalia nearly succeeded, review finds', *New York Times*, 25 Oct. 1993, p. A10.

* This chapter should not be considered as an official expression of US policy. All interpretations, conclusions, errors or omissions are the author's.

II. Competing foreign policy tendencies

Any nation contemplating a role in peace support operations must consider how far it is willing to commit itself to a community of interests transcending national borders and to employ its military to advance those interests. It is these very considerations which historically have occasioned sharp and recurring disagreements in the USA. In his recent review of *The Cambridge History of American Foreign Relations*, Professor Ernest May identifies several competing long-term tendencies in the USA concerning foreign relations. While cautioning against oversimplification, he singles out those represented by John Quincy Adams on the one hand and Thomas Jefferson and Woodrow Wilson on the other. Building on the example set by George Washington, Adams called for firm commitment to internal improvements and counselled against foreign entanglements even when the independence of other nations was in the balance. In contrast, Jefferson and Wilson wanted the USA to participate actively in a community of mutually supportive democratic nations. Wilson went further when proposing that they organize formally to maintain peace and advance democracy. May concludes that 'The aftermath of the Cold War . . . finds these competing conceptions still alive.'[3]

May adds that in the context of this historical competition there were recurring disputes about when the USA should resort to military force. Such disputes occasioned '[s]ome of the fiercest contention' among Americans with the '[n]ext in ferocity [being] contention over economic coercion'.[4]

There was, of course, remarkable internal agreement for much of the cold war that the USA should commit itself to the defence of far-flung states in Europe and Asia, but that agreement was due to circumstances which no longer obtain. The period of bipartisan foreign policy, as it was termed, reflected near-obsession with the perceived ideological and politico-military threat from the Soviet Union and the People's Republic of China. Walter Rostow captured some of that spirit when he wrote about the impact of the launching of Sputnik in 1957:

---

[3] May, E., '"Who are we?": two centuries of American foreign relations', *Foreign Affairs*, vol. 73, no. 2 (Mar./Apr. 1994), p. 136.

[4] May (note 3), p. 136.

There is no clear analogy in American history to the crisis triggered by [its] launching . . . This intrinsically harmless act of science and engineering was also . . . a powerful act of psychological warfare. It immediately set in motion forces in American political life which radically reversed the nation's ruling conception of its military problem.[5]

Concerned as well about a Soviet/communist threat to outflank the West by fomenting instabilities in the 'Third World', President John F. Kennedy in his inaugural address verbalized US determination to 'pay any price, bear any burden, meet any hardship, support any friend or oppose any foe to assure the survival and success of liberty'.

The Kennedy and early Johnson eras were perhaps a high point in the willingness of the public to use or threaten the use of US forces to support others in distant lands. The experience of the war in Viet Nam eroded that willingness and laid the foundations for the Nixon and Weinberger doctrines. Shortly after becoming president, Richard Nixon effectively called back Kennedy's pledge to 'pay any price' if it meant deploying military forces, particularly ground elements, to help defend others. When explaining his policy, he referred not only to material concerns, but to psychological ones as well: 'To contribute our predominant contribution [to the defence of others] might not have been beyond our physical resources . . . But it certainly would have exceeded our psychological resources'.[6] At the end of 1984 Caspar Weinberger, as Defense Secretary, took issue with Secretary of State George Shultz's willingness to advocate the use of force. Assisted by military officers whose memories had been seared by the experience of Viet Nam, Weinberger crafted the following guidelines:

1. Do not commit combat forces overseas unless the engagement is deemed vital to our national interests or that of our allies.

2. If combat troops are committed, do so wholeheartedly, with the clear intention of winning.

3. We should have clearly defined political and military objectives.

4. We should know precisely how our forces can accomplish the mission, and the relationship between forces and objectives must be continually re-assessed.

5. There should be reasonable assurance of public support.

---

[5] Rostow, W. W., *The United States in the World Arena* (Harper & Row: New York, 1960), p. 366.

[6] *US Foreign Policy for the 1970s: Building for Peace: A Report to the Congress by Richard Nixon, President of the United States*, 25 Feb. 1971, p. 11.

6. The commitment of combat forces abroad should be a last resort.[7]

A corollary to these principles, associated in particular with General Colin Powell, is emphasis on the employment of overwhelming or clearly decisive force—as seen in the US invasion of Grenada and Panama and in the Persian Gulf War.

This is the broad context of the formulation of PDD 25. Among the more specific conditioning factors was a general ambivalence which US policy makers have had and continue to have (perhaps increasingly) about the United Nations.

III. Ambivalence towards the UN

The USA was solidly in the forefront of efforts to establish the League of Nations as well as the UN, but in both cases it drew back— so far back in the former instance that it never joined. Cold war East– West tensions and deadlock in the Security Council—ironically the result of a veto power which the USA had itself advocated—convinced those responsible for foreign policy to put greater faith in collective defence than in collective security. The changed make-up of the UN, as more developing countries joined, also gave rise to North– South disagreements about the distribution of power in the UN and the priorities to be given to the Third World's agenda. In the 1970s and 1980s in particular, administration and congressional spokespersons complained that the UN was an unfriendly environment and that its methods and processes should be significantly reformed.

Possibly because President George Bush had served as US Ambassador to the UN, his administration's criticism of the organization seemed more muted than that of President Ronald Reagan's, but his spokespersons were no less insistent on the need for structural reform of the Secretariat and various agencies. Not surprisingly, however, the aftermath of the Gulf War caused a turn-around in expressed confidence. Bush's August 1991 *National Security Strategy* document referred to a 'new United Nations' that was 'beginning to act as it was designed' and needed strengthening to meet its potential.[8] His next and final *National Security Strategy* described the UN as a 'central

---

[7] Weinberger, C., 'The uses of military power', Speech to the National Press Club, Washington, DC, 28 Nov. 1984.

[8] *National Security of the United States* (The White House: Washington, DC, Aug. 1991), p. 13.

instrument for the prevention and resolution of conflicts and the preservation of peace' and stated that the USA would pay its full dues and take 'an active role in the full spectrum of UN peacekeeping and humanitarian relief planning and support'.[9] Congressional and other critics of the UN receded into the background.

As for peacekeeping *per se*, all concerned had agreed during the cold war that neither superpower should participate except in a supporting role—such as providing airlift or specialized equipment—or with a few individuals assigned to small operations such as UNTSO. Those restrictions were lifted as well after the Gulf War. In particular, President Bush responded to an internationally felt need to deal with the starving in Somalia by undertaking the UNITAF mission; this, however, was a UN-sanctioned but not UN-commanded operation, involving large numbers of troops under US control and with an exit date (which was not met) specified at the start.

That date was 20 January 1993, the day President Bill Clinton assumed office and the responsibility for directing US foreign policy.

IV. President Clinton and foreign policy

The key to understanding what led this particular president to issue PDD 25 as it finally appeared is that domestic policy is by far his foremost concern. His rise to the presidency was through the governmental and gubernatorial ranks of a very small state. Imperfect but nevertheless telling indicators of his priorities are statements by his foreign policy team that they manage to get the president to dedicate one hour a week to the subject.[10] One Democratic Party foreign policy scholar provided yet another way of putting it when he stated that the president's 'top foreign policy priority is health care reform'.[11]

President Clinton's domestic focus matches the mood of the nation, which treats foreign policy as an irritant, as something which gets in the way of dealing with fundamental concerns about jobs, taxes, health care, crime and the like:

[9] *National Security of the United States* (The White House: Washington, DC, Jan. 1993), p. 7.

[10] Hunt, A. R., 'There is no Clinton foreign policy', *Wall Street Journal,* 21 Apr. 1994, p. 17.

[11] Kondracke, M., 'UN speech aside, Clinton foreign policy still murky', *Roll Call,* 30 Sep. 1993.

Shortly after . . . Clinton took office he held a town meeting in Chillicothee, Ohio, during which an audience chosen by lottery asked him about everything . . . from health care to Hillary. But in the 90 minutes he did not get a single question on foreign policy . . . In all the town meetings [he] has held since . . . you could count on one hand the number of unprompted foreign policy questions he has received from the public.[12]

That the president is a devotee of domestic policy does not mean that he has no foreign policy views. When campaigning he was more hawkish than President Bush on air strikes in Bosnia and Herzegovina and called for a UN rapid deployment force that 'could be used for purposes beyond traditional peacekeeping, such as guarding the borders of countries threatened by aggression, preventing attacks on civilians, providing humanitarian relief, and combating terrorism and drug trafficking'.[13] In his inaugural address he spoke along the same lines but on a higher plane: 'When our vital interests are challenged, or the will of the international community is defied, we will act . . . with force if necessary'.[14] No doubt with his approval, in June 1993 his Ambassador to the UN, Madeleine Albright, advocated 'assertive multilateralism' to help 'failed societies . . . in the interests of their people and of international peace and security'.[15]

Within a few months that sense of assertiveness had waned considerably as the president and his foreign policy team launched a concerted effort to lower expectations about peacekeeping in general and US ground participation in particular.[16] A major event was the president's 27 September 1993 speech to the UN General Assembly when

[12] Friedman, T. L., 'There's nothing like foreign policy for producing ennui', *New York Times,* 13 June 1993, section 4, p. 3.

[13] On Bosnia and Herzegovina, see Klare, M., 'Know them by their enemies: Clinton and Bush on foreign policy', *The Nation,* vol. 255, no. 13 (26 Oct. 1992); and Cooper, M. *et al.,* '10 key decisions for the next president', *US News and World Report,* vol. 113, no. 15 (19 Oct. 1992). On a UN rapid deployment force, see Kramer, M., 'The political interest: Clinton's foreign policy jujitsu', *Time,* 30 Mar. 1992.

[14] Quoted in Horwitz, P. F., 'Clinton takes office, calling for renewal', *Inetrnational Herald Tribune,* 21 Jan. 1993. Emphasis added.

[15] US Congress, Statement by Madeleine K. Albright, in 'US participation in United Nations peacekeeping activities', *Hearings, House Committee on Foreign Affairs, Subcommittee on International Security, International Organizations and Human Rights* (US Government Printing Office: Washington, DC, 24 June 1993).

[16] See, for example, items cited in note 2 dating from Sep. 1993 and after; Gellmann, B., 'US reconsiders putting GIs under UN', *Washington Post,* 22 Sep. 1993, p. 1; and Lake, A., 'Yes to an American role in peacekeeping, but with conditions', *International Herald Tribune,* 7 Feb. 1994, p. 4. See also the Reuter report which appeared after the promulgation of PDD 25: 'Clinton defends limiting commitments of US troops abroad', *Washington Post,* 29 May 1994, p. 15.

he advised that the UN would have to learn 'to say "No"', that is, be more selective, when contemplating whether to deploy peacekeeping forces. Although PDD 25 did not appear until early May 1994, it had been signalled ahead of time.

Why the transition from a policy of assertiveness to one of caution? What happened is not difficult to explain: a White House determined to push its domestic agenda fell prey to the recurring difficulties faced by the UN and its forces in Somalia and Bosnia and Herzegovina and to sharp domestic disagreements over the assertiveness policy. Some disagreement came from the Pentagon. Faced with budget cuts and downsizing, military leaders feared having ground troops bogged down materially and morally in the midst of belligerents more eager to kill than to accommodate one another. Some in the military were also quite sceptical of the effectiveness of air strikes to influence the belligerents in any lasting way.[17]

More important, however, was the opposition from Congress and the sense that public opinion fundamentally would not approve US involvement in costly missions with little prospect of quick and lasting success.

V. Congress and public opinion

The relationship between Congress and the executive branch on peacekeeping is well summarized in the 1994 report of the Working Group on Peacekeeping and US National Interest, co-chaired by Senator Nancy Kassenbaum and Representative Lee Hamilton:

As the members of the United Nations have extended the scope of the world's organization peace operations, and the costs of American participation have risen, the role of UN peace operations in US policy has become a serious issue between the legislative and executive branches. If the two branches don't heal this division . . . efforts to improve the UN's effectiveness in peace operations will be derailed by US domestic discord.[18]

[17] Pfaff, W., 'The civilians overrule the Pentagon', *Baltimore Sun*, 14 Apr. 1994, p. 14; Gordon, M. R., 'Pentagon is wary of role in Bosnia', *New York Times*, 15 Mar. 1994, p. A1; and Sciolino, E., 'US military split on using air power against the Serbs', *New York Times*, 29 Apr. 1994, p. A1.
[18] *Peacekeeping and US National Interest: Report of the Working Group* (Henry L. Stimson Center: Washington, DC, 1994), p. 16.

Senior and influential legislators such as Senators Sam Nunn, Robert Byrd and Robert Dole and Representatives Thomas Foley, Richard Gephardt, Lee Hamilton, Robert Michel and Newt Gingrich have publicly warned the White House about the need for caution and strict limits in committing US ground troops to peace operations.[19] Even 'liberal internationalists' such as Senators Claiborne Pell and Joseph Biden have weighed in; for example, although the USA agreed to provide about 50 per cent of the troops necessary to help implement a general peace agreement in Bosnia and Herzegovina, Senator Pell continued to argue that that percentage was far too high.[20] Congress also registered its lack of enthusiasm for peacekeeping by refusing in separate votes to rid the USA of its arrears to the UN's peacekeeping account, to create a special $30 million fund that would have facilitated US participation in peacekeeping, or to build a command centre at the UN and train foreign peacekeepers.[21]

A number of factors underlie congressional opposition. The Kassenbaum–Hamilton report finds the disagreements on peacekeeping 'symptomatic of larger problems—differing opinions between the executive and legislative branches on the relative importance for foreign and domestic needs and the direction of foreign policy in general, as well as specific doubts about the United Nations and its implications for US security'.[22] On the latter, congressmen have expressed fears of outsiders dictating US policy or commanding US troops in risky operations.[23] They also fear open-ended commitments, not only when US troops are committed but also when they are not, since the US assessment for UN peacekeeping calls for it to pay

---

[19] See, for example, Bedard, P. and Gertz, B., 'Senators seek Bosnia resolution: bipartisan effort urges vote authorizing military action', *Washington Post* (5 May 1993); Ottoway, D. B., 'Hill leaders wary of Bosnia plan', *Washington Post*, 6 May 1993; Krauss, C., 'Many in Congress, citing Vietnam, oppose attacks', *New York Times*, 28 Apr. 1993, p. A10; Krauss, C., 'White House tries to calm Congress', *New York Times*, 6 Oct. 1993, p. A16; and Friedman, T., 'Seeking a balance: calls for pullout grow in Congress after losses in Mogadishu raid', *New York Times*, 6 Oct. 1993, p. 1.

[20] Binder, D., 'Senators criticize Bosnia aid plan', *New York Times*, 6 Oct. 1993, p. A8.

[21] 'House votes against UN peacekeeping fund', *Washington Times*, 14 Sep. 1993, p. 4; Rogers, E., 'House strips Pentagon budget of funds for future peacekeeping operations', *Wall Street Journal*, 1 Oct. 1993, p. 4; Strobel, W., 'UN peacekeeping cries for big bucks', *Washington Times*, 10 Mar. 1994, p. 13; and Devroy, A., 'Clinton signs new guidelines for UN peacekeeping', *Washington Post*, 6 May 1994, p. A32.

[22] *Peacekeeping and the US National Interest* (note 18), p. 16.

[23] See, for example, Williams, D., 'Joining the pantheon of American missteps', *Washington Post*, 26 Mar. 1994, p. 18; Novak, R., 'Blue helmets for Americans', *Washington Post*, 25 Apr. 1994, p. 16; and Devroy (note 21), pp. A1 and A32.

nearly one-third of the costs. As Senator Robert Byrd put it, 'Where will these funds come from? We . . . should not cut domestic spending to pay for these foreign adventures'.[24] His reference to domestic concerns brings to mind the telling observation of former House Speaker Thomas O'Neill that 'All politics is local'. At a national level, no organizations are more sensitive to public opinion than the Congress and the White House, and both seem to have concluded that the US public wants a very cautious and deliberate approach.[25]

VI. Peacekeeping and public opinion

Polling data, which admittedly fluctuate and can be difficult to interpret, suggest several conclusions. First, most Americans are generally not well informed about foreign affairs. For example, an early 1994 *Times Mirror* poll indicated that only 13 per cent of the respondents could identify UN Secretary-General Boutros Boutros-Ghali and only 28 per cent could name the Serbs as 'the ethnic group which had conquered much of Bosnia'.[26] Second, if polling data are representative, then a majority or near majority generally approves of the UN, of UN peacekeeping and of US participation in peacekeeping, including operations where force may have to be used for humanitarian purposes. A March 1994 *New York Times* poll of 1107 people indicated that 89 per cent believed that it was somewhat or extremely important to cooperate with other countries through the UN, 63 per cent believed the UN should send military troops to enforce peace plans in trouble spots, and 59 per cent believed that the USA has a responsibility to contribute troops to such operations.[27] These data are not inconsistent with those of a February 1994 University of Maryland poll of 700 people.[28] Between 81 and 83 per cent favoured the idea of UN peacekeeping operations 'in the event of

---

[24] Byrd, R. C., 'The perils of peacekeeping', *New York Times,* 19 Aug. 1993, p. 23.

[25] See, for example, Byrd (note 24); 'War Powers Act called unlawful, but not apt to go', *Washington Times,* 4 May 1993, p. 6; Hunt (note 10), p. 17; and 'White House criticized for reliance on polls', *Providence Journal–Bulletin,* 14 Apr. 1994, p. A8.

[26] Chart in *Time,* 28 Mar. 1994, p. 22.

[27] Survey data provided to the author by Edward Luck, President of the United Nations Association of the USA. See also Luck, E., 'The case for engagement: American interests in UN peace operations', eds D. C. F. Daniel and B. C. Hayes, *Beyond Traditional Peacekeeping* (Macmillan: London, 1995).

[28] Program on International Policy Studies, University of Maryland, News Release, 18 Feb. 1994.

large-scale atrocities' or 'gross human rights violations' and 67 per cent favoured them 'in a civil war when the combatants want help'; 49 per cent favoured the USA contributing troops 'in most cases' and 42 per cent 'in exceptional cases that directly affect US interests'. An April poll by the same organization, again of 700 people, showed that 66 per cent favoured 'contributing US troops to the existing UN peacekeeping force in Bosnia and Herzegovina to deliver humanitarian aid and monitor safe havens' and 56 per cent favoured 'sending a very large force of ground troops, including US troops, to occupy contested areas and forcibly stop ethnic cleansing'.[29] Interestingly, 63 per cent favoured 'contributing US troops to a UN peacekeeping force of 8000–10 000 to police the new agreement between the Bosnian Government and the Croats', although only 56 per cent favoured 'having Congress authorize the money for the USA to pay its share of the costs'. In addition, respondents exhibited 'ambivalence about involvement in Bosnia': 59 per cent did not wish to 'risk a repeat of the same mess we got ourselves into in Somalia' and 41 per cent accepted that the USA 'might get bogged down in another Vietnam'.

Policy makers seem to have latched on to public ambivalence. Noting that polling data supported the deployment of US troops to Bosnia and Herzegovina, the *Wall Street Journal* added that 'Pentagon officials and NATO allies worry that public and Congressional support would crumble as soon as the US suffered any deaths'.[30] Polling and anecdotal evidence give credence to these concerns. For example, after 18 US Rangers were killed in Mogadishu on 3 October 1993, a University of Maryland poll of 803 citizens showed that 28 per cent favoured immediate withdrawal, 43 per cent favoured withdrawal by 31 March (the date specified by the president), and only 27 per cent favoured staying until 'we have stabilized the country, even if this takes longer than six months'.[31] Even more important for US policy is what constituents tell their representatives. A flood of calls made to Senator Bill Bradley's office after the Ranger incident was 'overwhelmingly in favor of withdrawing US forces'

[29] Program on International Policy Studies, University of Maryland, News Release, 11 Apr. 1994.
[30] 'US officials fear that public backing for Bosnia peacekeeping is tenuous', *Wall Street Journal*, 11 Mar. 1994, p. 1.
[31] Morrison, D. C., 'Vietnam syndrome survives', *National Journal*, vol. 25, no. 4 (30 Oct. 1993).

from Somalia; Senator John McCain's office received 402 calls in one day, 400 of them favouring immediate withdrawal.[32]

In the light of all the above, it should not be surprising that PDD 25 embodies a highly cautious and deliberate approach to UN and US involvement in peace support operations.

VII. Summary of PDD 25

The unclassified version of the document contains six sections, the longest of which lays out the factors which the administration says it will consider when making decisions at three levels: whether or not to support the establishment of a UN or regionally sponsored operation; whether US personnel should participate in an approved operation; and whether they ought to participate significantly in enforcement missions where combat is likely.

The following are the criteria to be applied at the first level:[33]

– UN involvement advances US interests and there is an international community of interests for dealing with the problem on a multilateral basis.
– There is a threat to or breach of international peace and security . . . defined as one or a combination of the following: international aggression, or; urgent humanitarian disaster coupled with violence, [or] sudden interruption of established democracy or gross violation of human rights coupled with violence or the threat of violence.
– There are clear objectives and an understanding of where the mission fits . . . between traditional peacekeeping and peace enforcement.
– For traditional (Chapter VI) peacekeeping . . . a cease-fire should be in place and the consent of the parties obtained before the force is deployed.
– For peace enforcement (Chapter VII) . . . the threat to international peace and security is considered significant.
– The means to accomplish the mission are available, including the forces, financing, and mandate appropriate to the mission.
– The political, economic, and humanitarian consequences of inaction . . . are considered unacceptable.
– The operation's anticipated duration is tied to clear objectives and realistic criteria for ending the mission.

---

[32] Caption under photograph, *New York Times,* 7 Oct. 1993, p. A10; and Krauss, C., 'White House tries to calm Congress', *New York Times,* 6 Oct. 1993, p. A16.
[33] Quotations taken from US Department of State (note 1), pp. 4–5, 9, 10.

Additional more rigorous standards are identified for deciding on participation of US personnel in an operation:

   – Participation advances US interests and . . . the . . . risks . . . are considered acceptable.
     – Personnel, funds, and other resources are available.
     – US participation is necessary for . . . success.
     – The role of US forces is tied to clear objectives and an endpoint for US participation can be identified.
     – Domestic and Congressional support . . . can be marshalled.
     – Command and control arrangements are acceptable.

Finally, even more rigorous standards are laid out when there is a possibility of significant US participation in enforcement missions where combat is likely to occur. Specifically, there must be:

     – a determination to commit sufficient forces to achieve clearly defined objectives;
     – a plan to achieve those objectives decisively; [and]
     – a commitment to reassess and adjust, as necessary, the size, composition, and disposition of our forces.

Among the second-level criteria is one which calls for acceptable command and control arrangements. PDD 25 devotes a whole section to this issue. It makes clear that US troops will always remain under US command but leaves open the possibility of operational control by a non-US 'competent UN commander'. By operational control is meant the assignment of tasks to US forces for a specific mission or during a specific time-frame. The foreign commander is proscribed, however, from 'chang[ing] the mission or deploy[ing] US forces outside the area of responsibility agreed to by the President' of the USA, nor is he allowed to 'separate units, divide their supplies, administer discipline, promote anyone, or change their internal organization'.

Two conditions will almost automatically limit the extent to which the USA will agree to place forces under UN operational control. One is the extent of participation by US forces: the greater their role, the less likely it is that the USA will give up control. A second obtains when US forces participate 'in a major peace enforcement mission that is likely to involve combat'. Such a mission 'should ordinarily be conducted under US command and operational control or through competent regional organizations such as NATO or ad hoc coalitions'.

The remainder of PDD 25 focuses on the role of regional organizations, on the need to reduce mission costs and on measures to strengthen the UN's ability to manage peace operations and the USA's ability to support them. On regional organizations, US policy accepts the appropriateness of peace operations by regional organizations while emphasizing that the UN remains the primary body with the authority to conduct them. On cost reductions, the document calls for implementation of various measures within the UN including the establishment of an Inspector-General's office. It also makes clear US determination to see a reduction of its share of the UN's peace operations budget from 31.7 per cent to 25 per cent, adding that the Congress is ready to force the issue, probably by refusing to fund more than 25 per cent after fiscal year 1995. Suggestions to strengthen the UN focus on reconfiguring and expanding the Department of Peacekeeping Operations in the UN Secretariat, establishing rapid reaction teams and capabilities (such as a modest airlift capability through pre-negotiated contracts), establishing a Peace Operations Training Program, and setting out ways in which the USA can assist in such endeavours on a reimbursable basis. Finally, suggestions for strengthening US support focus particularly on how the Departments of Defence and State should share responsibilities.

VIII. Conclusion

In sum, PDD 25 contains numerous guidelines for making decisions about peace operations and US participation in them and recommends measures for improving the conduct of operations and associated UN and US capabilities. Fundamentally, it 'aims to ensure that our use of peacekeeping is *selective* and *more effective*'.[34]

Its highly cautious and deliberate approach reflects a restrictive domestic context. Deep-rooted competing tendencies within the body politic about the USA's role in foreign policy and contentions about the use of force are part of the explanatory context. They were evident not only in the differing views between power centres in Washington, but also over time in one power centre, the White House. The new President Clinton was markedly more enthusiastic about the possibilities of peacekeeping than the later Clinton who, committed to his

[34] US Department of State (note 1), p. 3. Emphasis in original.

overriding domestic agenda, found himself beset by peacekeeping concerns including opposition from influential congressmen.

Public opinion may have been the decisive factor. An Adamsian concern for domestic improvement and for avoiding foreign entanglements seems to run below the surface of an otherwise generally supportive Jeffersonian public attitude towards the UN and peace operations. Sensing that concern, political leaders at both ends of Pennsylvania Avenue seem unconvinced that the public would sustain support for operations which may be costly and protracted. It is now a cliché to say that Clinton's is a minimalist foreign policy in tune with a public which voted for him because he represented domestic change.[35] PDD 25 fits that pattern.

---

[35] Friedman, T. L., 'Theory vs. practice: Clinton's stated foreign policy turns into more modest "self-containment"', *New York Times*, 1 Oct. 1993, p. A2.

6. Other new and emerging peacekeepers

*Angela Kane**

I. Introduction

This chapter examines the motivations and policies of selected new and emerging troop contributors. Some are not strictly new peacekeepers but states which have substantially increased their participation since the end of the cold war. Of the permanent members of the UN Security Council, China and France are considered.[1] Various other contributors which are not permanent members of the Security Council are then examined, grouped by region. Countries have been selected on the basis of recent or potential troop contributions or because of expectations on the part of the international community that they should participate in multilateral efforts to keep the peace.

II. China: strict observance of Charter principles

China has maintained a conspicuously low profile in Security Council debates on peacekeeping and as a troop contributor. Only in 1988 did it become a member of the General Assembly's Special Committee on Peace-keeping Operations. Its position emerged more clearly during the 1990–91 Iraq–Kuwait crisis. Following its strong condemnation of Iraq's invasion, China abstained on Resolution 678 which on 29 November 1990 authorized 'all necessary measures' to resolve the crisis if Iraq failed to withdraw unconditionally from Kuwait, believing that the crisis must be resolved peacefully and that resorting to military action would have an adverse effect not only on the region but also on global peace and security. Since then, however, China has

[1] Individual studies of Russia and the USA are presented in chapters 4 and 5, respectively, in this volume.

* The views expressed are those of the author and do not necessarily reflect those of the United Nations. This chapter incorporates passages from a paper written for the US Naval War College, Rhode Island, Feb. 1994 and published as 'Other selected states: motivations and factors in national choices', eds D. Daniel and B. C. Hayes, *Beyond Traditional Peacekeeping* (Macmillan: London, 1995). The author acknowledges the assistance of Anneli Berntsson, Research Assistant, SIPRI Project on Peacekeeping and Regional Security, in updating this version of her paper.

increasingly joined the consensus on resolutions authorizing UN operations.

China has continued to stress the Charter's provisions for the peaceful settlement of international disputes and has welcomed the strengthening of the UN's role in preventive diplomacy. Vice-Premier Qian Qichen in his address to the General Assembly on 29 September 1993 urged observance of the basic principles of the Charter, namely respect for sovereignty and non-interference in the internal affairs of member states, and underlined the importance of regional organizations which, he said, should assume greater responsibility for maintaining peace and security. In the debate on peacekeeping the Chinese representative reinforced these views: 'at any time and under any circumstances, the consent and cooperation from the relevant governments or parties must be obtained . . . in carrying out these operations, the UN must adopt a neutral, fair and impartial approach and in no way get involved in the internal conflict of a country'. He criticized the 'indiscriminate use of sanctions or force' in the name of the UN, yet considered that the UN operation in Cambodia had provided 'useful experience'.[2] China believes that UN peacekeeping, if used properly (that is, following the Charter's principles), 'will play an increasingly important role', and China 'is ready to make further contributions to the UN peacekeeping activities through its active involvement'.

The first Chinese peacekeepers were those deployed to UNIKOM in 1992. By 1994, 60 Chinese military observers were serving with UNTSO in the Middle East, with UNIKOM and in Western Sahara, Mozambique and Liberia.[3] Their numbers were small but they contributed to the multilateral character of the operations and manifested the Chinese desire to participate. Consistent with China's belief in regional efforts, the largest Chinese commitment so far has been to UNTAC with 400 troops and 46 military observers.

It is unlikely that Chinese participation in UN peacekeeping will notably increase in the near future unless an operation is mounted in Asia—to which China would feel compelled to contribute in a more than symbolic way. Barring a major policy shift China is likely to

---

[2] Statement by Mr Zhang Yan, Representative of China, in the Fourth Committee of the General Assembly on agenda item 87, 'Comprehensive review of the whole question of peace-keeping operations in all their aspects', New York, 24 Nov. 1993, UN document A/C.4/48/SR.22.

[3] UN, 'United Nations peace-keeping', *Information Notes Update*, Dec. 1994.

continue to contribute a handful of military observers (rather than troops) and only to those operations which meet its criteria. Neither domestic public opinion, lack of training and experience nor financial concerns appears to have any significant impact on China's decision to participate or not. If, however, the international community comes to feel that China should contribute peacekeeping troops in larger numbers, considerable pressure will have to be applied to convince it to do so. In view of its rapidly growing economy and military budget,[4] it would not be unreasonable to expect China to assume a larger share of responsibility for carrying out the decisions which it jointly takes with other Security Council members.[5]

III. France: strong political engagement

France, which in 1948 had participated in one of the earliest peace-keeping missions, UNTSO, and then in the 1960s had rejected the idea of peacekeeping operations and refused to pay its peacekeeping assessments, became in the early 1990s a committed participant. By the end of 1994 it was contributing a total of 5023 troops to seven operations, 90 per cent of them in the former Yugoslavia.[6]

France's first participation after UNTSO was in UNIFIL starting in 1978, followed by UNTAG in Namibia in 1989–90. Following the conclusion of the Paris Agreements on Cambodia in October 1992, France became a large-scale troop contributor to UNTAC, having contributed significantly to the international effort to bring democracy to Cambodia. France was also the first country to offer a contingent of stand-by troops to the UN. In the course of 1992 it became the leading participant in peacekeeping operations. France has paid a heavy price: 45 of its soldiers had been killed in Bosnia and Herzegovina alone by August 1995.[7]

A year later, setbacks prompted the Foreign Minister, Alain Juppé, to refer to 'new kinds of uncertainty and disorder' and to list three guiding principles on which France's foreign policy was based: desire for independence, commitment to its fundamental interests and devotion to law and justice. In the former Yugoslavia France at one point

---

[4] Bergstrand, B.-G. *et al.*, 'World military expenditure', *SIPRI Yearbook 1994* (Oxford University Press: Oxford, 1994), pp. 441–48.

[5] See also Kristof, N. D., 'The rise of China', *Foreign Affairs*, Nov./Dec. 1993, pp. 59–74.

[6] 'United Nations peace-keeping' (note 3).

[7] Information provided by the French Embassy, Stockholm.

had double the number of troops of the next-largest contributor and it was the only country to send reinforcements for the security of the safe areas declared by the Security Council in June 1993. In view of this commitment, France firmly rejects any challenge to its authority in peacekeeping matters:

The efforts [France] has made entitle it to tell those who have been free with their advice and lessons that they might be better heard if they were agreeing, when they are able to do so, to commit their own troops to the field. Once in contact with the realities of the situation, they would undoubtedly better appreciate the fact that between negotiated peace and chaos there is no middle ground.[8]

France has taken the high moral ground on a number of questions ranging from troop contributions to financial matters.[9] Its engagement has been pragmatic and without the dogma that usually surrounds foreign policy initiatives, as demonstrated in a comprehensive report on French participation in peacekeeping operations, the Trucy Report, prepared at the request of Prime Minister Édouard Balladur in February 1994.[10]

Part of the reason for France's strong engagement is undoubtedly its distrust of US intentions in Europe. With the disappearance of the Warsaw Pact and the decline of NATO's foremost security role, France has stepped up efforts to contribute to a European collective security policy, while at the same time showing an interest in a transformed transatlantic alliance, which France would help shape and define as well as fully participate in.[11]

Another side to France's motivation is its search for influence, rank and grandeur. The Trucy Report is sprinkled with recommendations on how best to exploit France's high level of engagement (including not letting the Nordic countries determine peacekeeping 'dogma'). Although the report cites the high costs which France incurs for its

[8] Address by Foreign Minister Alain Juppé to the UN General Assembly, New York, 29 Sep. 1993.

[9] France has had a consistent record of paying its assessed contributions within the specified time-limit (i.e., before 31 Jan. each year).

[10] Trucy, F., Parlementaire en Mission, Rapport au Premier Ministre: Participation de la France aux opérations maintien de la paix, août 1993–février 1994 [Report to the Prime Minister: France's participation in peacekeeping operations, Aug. 1993–Feb. 1994] (in French. Unpublished).

[11] See also Asmus, R. D., Kugler, R. L. and Larrabee, F. S., 'Building a new NATO', *Foreign Affairs*, vol. 72, no. 4 (Sep./Oct. 1993), pp. 28–40.

troops in addition to the assessments levied by the UN, participation in peacekeeping operations is never questioned, but rather presented as a source of pride and accomplishment as well as necessity.[12]

France's high profile and the priority it gives to UN peacekeeping are also the result of its wish to preserve its privileged status as a permanent member of the Security Council at a time when reform of the Council and expansion are being hotly debated. Another aspect is a degree of competition with the UK, also a permanent Security Council member, which has tried to take the lead in elaborating peacekeeping doctrine and thus to dominate the peacekeeping debate. This is resented by France, which is at a further disadvantage when such discussions take place, as English prevails at international meetings and French interventions are usually heard via interpretation. France has been tenacious, however, and, given all these considerations, its commitment to the UN and multilateral action can be expected to continue.

IV. Europe: Spain leads the way

After years of international semi-isolationism during the Franco regime, European Community membership became an important part of Spain's foreign policy, and participation in UN peacekeeping was a logical extension of this policy.

Spain's first participation was in UNTAG, quickly followed by ONUCA and ONUSAL. By the end of 1994 it had 1342 troops deployed in UN peacekeeping operations in El Salvador (16), Mozambique (40) and the former Yugoslavia (1286).[13] This pattern of contributions partly reflects Spain's foreign policy priorities which, because of historic and linguistic ties, lie with Central America, North Africa and Europe.[14] The Foreign Ministry points out, however, that future participation in peacekeeping operations may include other regions, specifically as a result of 'important interests' which Spain retains in Angola and Mozambique.[15]

---

[12] Trucy (note 10), p. 86.

[13] 'United Nations peace-keeping' (note 3).

[14] 'España y las OMPs de Naciones Unidas' [Spain and UN peacekeeping operations], Paper delivered by the Director-General for International Organizations, Ministry of Foreign Affairs, early 1994 (in Spanish. Unpublished conference paper).

[15] Military observers were stationed in Angola as part of UNAVEM I and II from 1989 to 1993 but withdrawn when a political settlement proved elusive.

Spain has played a leading role in Central America in helping to resolve regional conflicts, both alone and in concert with others. As one of the Friends of the Secretary-General for El Salvador, it contributed substantially to the settlement of the conflict and the implementation of the peace accords, the latter primarily by assisting in police monitoring and the establishment of a new national civil police.

As a result of its positive experience of these operations Spain sent troops to UNPROFOR in the former Yugoslavia, but it has consistently stressed the humanitarian mandate of its forces in Bosnia and Herzegovina. Voices were heard in early 1994 asking for the withdrawal of the Spanish forces[16] but Foreign Minister Javier Solana, on a visit to the front lines in February, said that he considered 'the possibility of a complete withdrawal very remote. The only aid that reaches the population is that escorted by the "blue helmets"'. Media coverage has generally been favourable towards and public opinion supportive of Spain's involvement in humanitarian missions. After an incident in Bosnia and Herzegovina which resulted in heavy casualties (Spain lost 11 soldiers, with others wounded), newspaper articles rang with patriotic fervour and the number of soldiers volunteering for UN duty immediately increased to four applications for every vacancy. A poll conducted in April 1994 found a majority in favour of sending troops on peacekeeping missions, with a higher percentage among those aged 18–29 supporting the 'blue helmets' enthusiastically.[17]

Exasperation at times shows through. In an interview in January 1994 Foreign Minister Solana warned that Spain would have to reconsider the deployment of its troops in Bosnia and Herzegovina if no progress towards an agreement was made: 'If the parties are still in conflict, if they don't want to be helped, there is no sense in continuing'.[18] Spain wants peacekeeping operations to be an integral part of the solution to crises, not a permanent fixture on the landscape. Hence Spain withdrew from UNAVEM II in December 1993.

Spain has been faced with the increasing cost of participation in UN missions. In 1991, at a time when peacekeeping costs started to skyrocket, it volunteered to move from assessment category C to B,

---

[16] *Diario 16*, 12 Dec. 1993; and *El País*, 14 Dec. 1993, p. 24, 22 Jan. 1994, p. 5, and 3 Feb. 1994, p. 14 (in Spanish).

[17] *El Mundo*, 3 Apr. 1994, p. 8 (in Spanish).

[18] Interview with radio station 'Onda Cero', 20 Dec. 1993.

which resulted in a quintupling of its financial contributions.[19] This was coupled with additional costs of deployment, as the UN rate of reimbursement only covers about one-third of the actual cost accruing to a developed country. Because of its severe economic crisis, Spain in 1993 fell behind in its payments for the first time.

Spain's armed forces had a poor reputation because of their governance of Spain under the Franco dictatorship. Today conscription and the NATO alliance are unpopular. Experience in multilateral missions is seen as positive. 'It gives the idea to the armed forces that they are more humane, and not just for fighting war', one Spanish military official explained. Experience is gained in training, language and cultural exposure, which is further enhanced by participating in various peace missions of the OSCE, NATO and the WEU.

Spain has undoubtedly gained prestige and influence in the international community as a member of the Security Council in 1993–94 and has used its presence in peacekeeping operations to obtain influence, to have its voice heard and to have an input into all major policy decisions. Spain challenges the dogma of the traditional peacekeepers, particularly the Nordic countries, and sees itself as a leader among the Ibero-American states, for which it recently established a training facility to prepare police forces for UN service. Given all these considerations Spain's commitment to UN peacekeeping is likely to continue.

V. Asia: diversity

Asia has always had several traditional troop contributors like India, Nepal and Pakistan, but new contributors are starting to emerge.

South Korea

Having joined the UN only in 1991, the Republic of Korea has set its sights on 'an opportunity to serve on the Security Council'[20] and demonstrated its commitment to multilateral action by sending, in the latter part of 1993, an engineering unit of 250 troops to UNOSOM II,

---

[19] Spain is assessed 1.98% of the peacekeeping budget, which amounted to $70 million in 1993. By comparison, in 1989 Spain was assessed $1.2 million.

[20] Address by Foreign Minister Sung-Joo Han to the General Assembly, New York, 29 Sep. 1993, UN document A/48/PV.9.

although the unstable situation there led to withdrawal earlier than expected. In August 1994 a medical contingent was sent to MINURSO. South Korea said that it would 'gradually increase [its] support' for peacekeeping operations 'commensurate with [its] ability to do so'.[21] Its commitment is motivated by its history and current geopolitical situation: 'Despite the worldwide trends towards peace and co-operation, there is still tension in Korea . . . the solution to the inter-Korean question should thus be sought in the context of the post-cold war international order of reconciliation and co-operation. This means active participation by both North and South Korea in the regional and global order'. It is not surprising therefore that Korea gives priority to 'a discussion on the role of the UN in preventive diplomacy directed towards defusing potential threats to international peace and security'.[22] By participating in UN missions, South Korea validates its own claim to multilateral assistance and asserts its role as a growing regional power.

Having survived a succession of authoritarian military governments, South Korea's democratic culture is fragile. Public opinion is untested, but is seen as being generally guarded as increased affluence has bred conservatism among a growing middle class concerned first and foremost with stability. While South Korea's forays into peacekeeping will most likely remain cautious, they will nevertheless continue and be increased where politically feasible and expeditious. South Korea could become a steady contributor to UN operations.

The ASEAN states[23]

Another promising prospect is offered by the seven ASEAN states. While ASEAN was established to focus on economic and social issues rather than security, the Cambodian conflict served as a catalyst in modifying this approach, and for many years provided the political glue that held it together. ASEAN's skilful management of the Cambodia issue at the UN, leading to the establishment of UNTAC, showed the efficacy of united efforts, giving it confidence and greater assertiveness in regional security affairs.

---

[21] Statement by Ambassador Chong-Ha Yoo before the Special Committee on Peace-keeping Operations, 22 Apr. 1993. Unpublished.

[22] Address by Foreign Minister Han (note 20).

[23] ASEAN was formed in 1968 by Indonesia, Malaysia, the Philippines, Singapore and Thailand. Brunei Darussalam joined in 1984 and Viet Nam in 1995.

Five ASEAN members participated in UNTAC,[24] but since then—with the exception of Malaysia which has increased its forces—ASEAN's presence has been negligible. As of 30 November 1994, Brunei Darussalam was not represented in any UN peacekeeping missions; the Philippines participated with 1 person, Indonesia with 297, Malaysia with 2844, Singapore with 6 and Thailand with 6.[25] While ASEAN has tried to elaborate a common approach to UN issues, including peacekeeping, differences in political views, geographical size and economic strength produce a diversity of approaches.[26] Brunei and Singapore, because of their small size and population, can never be other than symbolic contributors to UN operations, but for small countries the UN is an important forum. Singapore, in addition to sending well-trained and disciplined police personnel, has been active in the ongoing debate on peacekeeping philosophy and has been at the forefront of discussions on the enlargement of the Security Council. The Philippines is the economically weakest link in the ASEAN chain and continues to suffer from a foreign debt crisis and slow growth rates. A negative political image from the Marcos years lingers, and political instability was evident in several attempted coups against President Corazon Aquino and the continuing threat of a communist insurgency. While this situation is improving under President Fidel Ramos, it does not appear to be a propitious time for the Philippines to send armed forces abroad for peacekeeping missions.[27]

Thailand shares a border with Cambodia and has a long history of association with the Khmer Rouge. It was important to correct this negative image by participating in UNTAC. However, Thailand's assistance in such areas as mine clearance promptly ceased with UNTAC's withdrawal. Of the ASEAN countries Thailand has the largest military[28] and one which has dominated politics for decades.

---

[24] Viet Nam had not yet joined ASEAN. Of a total of some 22 000 personnel, ASEAN contributed 4385 (Brunei Darussalam, 3; Indonesia 2034; Malaysia 1208; the Philippines 351; Singapore 75; and Thailand 714).

[25] 'United Nations peace-keeping' (note 3).

[26] Statement on behalf of ASEAN by Ambassador Pibulsonggram before the Fourth Committee of the General Assembly on agenda item 87, 'Comprehensive review of the whole question of peace-keeping operations in all their aspects', 24 Nov. 1993 (note 2).

[27] As of 30 Nov. 1994 the Philippines had 1 civilian policeman in UNOSOM. See 'United Nations peace-keeping' (note 3).

[28] Total armed forces (at early 1995) stood at 283 000 for a population of 57.6 million. This compares to 272 000 for Indonesia, which has a population of 195.7 million, and

Together with Singapore it has initiated and organized a series of workshops on ASEAN–UN cooperation in peacekeeping and preventive diplomacy, but the emphasis has been on the latter, as Thailand views with misgiving recent UN forays into peace enforcement and military intervention in 'zones of instability and potential crisis'.[29] Deputy Foreign Minister Surin Pitsuwan has declared Thailand's willingness to set up a separate peacekeeping unit to respond to UN requests,[30] but it seems unlikely that Thailand will develop into a major contributor to UN operations.

Its neighbour Malaysia has shown increasing willingness to deploy its forces under the UN. A large contingent (1135) served in Somalia. By November 1994, 1603 troops were involved in Bosnia and Herzegovina and smaller numbers in five other UN operations.[31] In addition to Malaysia's often-stated 'strong and abiding commitment to a revitalized and strengthened UN in the post-cold war era', one motivation for its increased participation may be a wish to help fellow Muslims in Bosnia and Herzegovina, but the reasons are undoubtedly more complex and may be found in Malaysia's own history, particularly its experience of fusing a cluster of independent sultanates and ethnic groups into a multi-ethnic state and its recent rapid economic growth. All these have given Malaysia the confidence to speak out on international issues.

Malaysia has played an important role in furthering South–South cooperation and has stood up to the West in defending its views on the environment and on human rights. Malaysia considers that it has a contribution to make and sees itself as a champion of the developing world, which explains its strong presence in Somalia. It believes that the developed countries 'with their resources should assist developing countries to participate [in peacekeeping operations] by making available material resources'.[32] It has also criticized the developed countries:

---

121 300 for Malaysia, which has a population of 18.4 million. See *Asian Defence Journal*, vol. 25, no. 1 (1995), pp. 11, 15.

[29] UN, Improving the capacity of the United Nations for peace-keeping: Report of the Secretary-General, UN document A/48/403/Add.1, 2 Nov. 1993.

[30] 'Thailand ready to set up peacekeeping unit', *The Nation* (Bangkok), 20 Nov. 1993, p. 1.

[31] UNIKOM, UNAVEM, MINURSO, ONUMOZ and UNOMIL.

[32] Statement by Ambassador Razali Ismail to the Special Committee on Peacekeeping Operations, United Nations, New York, 30 Mar. 1994. Unpublished.

Developed countries with their resources should assist developing countries to participate [in peacekeeping operations] by making available material resources. We should not indulge in the cynical view that developing countries seek high-tech weapons through involvement in peacekeeping or that they participate to make money.[33]

It has demonstrated its willingness to back its words by action. When the death of a Malaysian soldier in far-away Somalia traumatized the population, the government was able to contain public emotion by declaring this to be part of its international duty.

Despite Malaysia's deep commitment to the UN, it would like to see a number of changes. In a statement on peacekeeping in November 1993 Razali Ismail, Ambassador to the UN, underlined that 'Malaysian peacekeeping troops were sent to Somalia to keep foodlines open and thereby help feed the people of Somalia. We did not acquiesce in any personalized undertaking seeking the arrest of any principal player'.[34] Malaysia considers the current Security Council composition and the veto undemocratic and demands 'that troop-contributing countries are kept closely informed and consulted on all major developments'.[35] It further emphasizes the need

to dispel perceptions that the Western-dominated Council increasingly resorts to questionable decisions, the implementation of which in the main are [sic] left to other member states, particularly from the Third World. Such perceptions draw their basis from peacekeeping operations, approved by the Council, and from which major countries gradually disassociate themselves for domestic reasons. Somalia can well be a case in point; a situation there may arise in the future when virtually troops of Third World countries only will be left there.[36]

This is unusually blunt language, but despite its criticism Malaysia has been steadfast in abiding by its commitment to the UN, increasing its troop strength in Somalia at a time when Western nations were

[33] Statement by Ambassador Razali Ismail (note 32).

[34] Statement by Ambassador Razali Ismail of Malaysia in the Fourth Committee of the General Assembly on agenda item 87, 'Comprehensive review of the whole question of peace-keeping operations in all their aspects', New York, 29 Nov. 1993, UN document A/C.4/48/SR.23.

[35] Malaysia considered this matter important enough to make a formal *démarche* to the President of the Security Council, urging the development 'of a practice or mechanism that would allow direct and close consultations between the Security Council and the countries contributing troops'. See UN document S/1994/120, 4 Feb. 1994.

[36] See note 35.

withdrawing *en bloc*. This commitment is likely to continue, given the strongly held views of the government and the overwhelming domestic support these policies enjoy.

For Indonesia peacekeeping is not high on the political agenda. None the less, it committed a large number of troops to UNTAC (which clashed with the UN command since they took orders from Jakarta rather than accepting the supremacy of the UN). At the end of 1994 the country had a total of 298 troops, civilian police and military observers in UNPROFOR, ONUMOZ, UNOSOM, UMOMIG and UNIKOM.[37] Since the Indonesian military is endowed with the dual functions of custodian of security and of socio-political stability in a country of 3000 islands and a large number of ethnic groups, not all of whom support the central government, the government's priority is stability at home. At the same time President Suharto, who calls himself the 'father of development' and has seen his country make great economic strides since he assumed the presidency in 1968, now feels more confident in assuming a higher profile in foreign affairs. As head of the largest Islamic nation and current chairman of the Non-Aligned Movement (NAM), Suharto has championed the rights of the Muslims of Bosnia and Herzegovina and tried to increase the NAM's relevance by giving it greater economic focus. Within ASEAN, rivalry between Indonesia and Malaysia has started to develop, with Indonesia resenting the outspokenness and increasing emancipation of Malaysian foreign policy. Both peoples being Malay, Indonesia has long considered itself the 'elder brother' and feels overshadowed by Malaysia's high profile in international affairs, including its participation in UN peacekeeping.

The only ASEAN country willing to contribute more than a token number of troops to UN operations at present is Malaysia. While economic prosperity has brought modernization of the armed forces of all ASEAN countries, the political will to make these forces available to the UN is lacking. Attempts to set up a regional ASEAN training centre for peacekeeping forces have not been successful. Some members have objected that military doctrines are different and joint training is thus not practical, although this idea continues to be promoted at the think-tank level.

The formal decision of the ASEAN summit meeting of January 1992 to give security cooperation high priority was an important shift

---

[37] 'United Nations peace-keeping' (note 3).

from ASEAN's previous focus on economic and political cooperation, although it is too early to expect practical results. Joint military exercises are confined to the bilateral and trilateral level and mechanisms for ASEAN defence cooperation lack definition, particularly as ASEAN was never conceived as a defence organization. While the value of training and experience to be gained through participation in UN peacekeeping operations is recognized, practical follow-up is lacking. This situation is unlikely to change in the next few years.

VI. Latin America: prospects for involvement

Latin American states have been members of the UN since its foundation and have thus participated in many UN operations, but except for Argentina, which has consistently provided troops, and to a lesser extent Chile they have seemed more reluctant to participate than the African countries and when they have done so their contingents have been largely symbolic. Their absence may be explained by preoccupation with development and social inequity, internal conflict, insurgency movements or the drug trade. Today, however, the international community is clearly looking to Latin American countries, now largely democratic and more prosperous, to assume their share of the increasingly heavy burden of peacekeeping.

Venezuela, Mexico and Brazil particularly are coming under closer scrutiny from other UN members. Apart from their economic power, they project a high political profile at the UN: Venezuela completed a two-year term on the Security Council in 1992–93, while Brazil was a member in 1993–94.

Venezuela

Venezuela's first ever participation was in UNIKOM, where it provided a handful of military observers. As of November 1994 only six Venezuelans were serving as military observers in four operations.[38] Considering its high profile in the Security Council, particularly regarding Bosnia and Herzegovina, its efforts to put the issue of Haiti onto the Council agenda and its highly visible role in the peace processes in El Salvador and Haiti as one of the four Friends of the

[38] UNIKOM (2), ONUSAL (1), MINURSO (1) and UNPROFOR (2). See 'United Nations peace-keeping' (note 3).

Secretary-General, more might be expected. It is anxious to enhance its international profile, but it is equally clear that this ambition is unlikely to be accompanied soon by the dispatch of larger numbers of troops to UN operations or increased financial contributions.

Venezuela's military has been weakened by a top-heavy structure, inter-service rivalries, lack of organizational goals and motivation during a long period of democratic rule, and a purge of the armed forces after the attempted military coup of February 1992. Other domestic woes are also likely to keep Venezuela preoccupied. Social discontent arising from the inequitable distribution of income and wealth after economic growth in the 1970s and 1980s and fiscal mismanagement have meant that the current government spends much effort on maintaining and consolidating its power and trying to contain domestic political unrest. Sending troops abroad would deplete the military force available for operations at home during a crucial period. Sending troops to UN operations or making additional financial contributions to UN efforts to settle conflicts abroad would also further alienate a population which feels that its government should concentrate on domestic difficulties.[39]

At the UN Venezuela has been critical of the Security Council's prerogatives: 'The large majority of UN Members does not participate in the decision-making process to authorize an operation, although they are being asked to participate and to contribute to the operations' financing'.[40] Taking into consideration this view as well as the domestic situation, it seems optimistic to expect a larger contribution from Venezuela to future UN peacekeeping.

Mexico

Mexico is another country that should be in a position to participate in more UN operations since, notwithstanding recent setbacks, it has made huge economic strides over the last decade and is very active at the UN. Even more forcefully than Venezuela, Mexico rejects the *modus operandi* of the Security Council and particularly the veto

[39] Foreign Minister Ochoa Antich, Address to the UN General Assembly, New York, 1 Oct. 1993, UN document A/48/PV.12.

[40] Statement by Ambassador Adolfo R. Taylhardat before the Fourth Committee of the General Assembly New York on agenda item 87, 'Comprehensive review of the whole question of peace-keeping operations in all their aspects', 30 Nov. 1993, UN document A/C4/48/SR.25.

power as being undemocratic. It also argues that instead of acting on behalf of its constituency the Council has increasingly come to monopolize the power ceded to it voluntarily by the UN membership.[41]

According to Mexico the Council's first priority should be the peaceful settlement of disputes. Its Foreign Minister told the General Assembly in 1993: 'The recent frequent recourse to the Security Council has tended to hide the fact that our first obligation is to resolve differences by peaceful means'.[42] Mexico believes in 'preventive peacekeeping', the focusing of UN efforts on economic and social development: 'Peacekeeping operations are the final recourse in the search for peace. We should admit that their proliferation is due to our failure [at] building a better and more just society'.[43] Mexico has tartly observed of traditional peacekeeping that 'we should recognize that the quantitative and qualitative build-up of such operations has not proportionally resulted in a more peaceful or more harmonious world'.[44]

In view of the Security Council's exclusive power to establish peacekeeping operations, Mexico, in consistency with the principle of 'no taxation without representation', considers that Council members have the prime responsibility for implementing its decisions, including providing the necessary troops. Yet in cases where Mexico is actively involved in the search for a peaceful settlement, its level of commitment is clearly higher. This was so in El Salvador, where the Mexican Government hosted the negotiations between the government of El Salvador and the FMLN (Frente Farabundo Martí para la Liberación Nacional), was one of the four Friends of the Secretary-General and acted as facilitator. ONUSAL, the subsequent UN operation, is the only one to which Mexico has deployed military observers; it has also extended cooperation and facilities for training the new civilian police of El Salvador. Similar involvement may occur in Guatemala now that negotiations between the government and the URNG (Unidad Revolucionaria Nacional Guatemalteca) have come to a successful first conclusion. As a neighbour, Mexico has again

---

[41] Address by Mr Fernando Solana, Foreign Minister of Mexico, to UN General Assembly, New York, 29 Sep. 1993, UN document A/48/PV.9.

[42] Address by Mr Fernando Solana (note 41).

[43] Statement by Mr Héctor Cárdenas Suárez to the Fourth Committee of the General Assembly on agenda item 87, 'Comprehensive review of the whole question of peace-keeping operations in all their aspects', New York, 29 Nov. 1993, UN document A/C.4/48/SR.24.

[44] Statement by Ambassador Daniel de la Pedraja to the UN Special Committee on Peacekeeping Operations, New York, 30 Mar. 199. Unpublished.

hosted the negotiations and shown a keen interest in settling this conflict. It may also be willing to contribute to the implementation of the agreements, although the involvement of neighbouring countries in peacekeeping operations is usually kept to a minimum in order to avoid cross-border friction.

Brazil

Some 30–40 years ago Brazil participated in two UN operations,[45] but it was only recently, following a period of impressive economic growth, two decades of authoritarian rule and its gradual return to democratic normalcy, that Brazil again joined the ranks of UN troop contributors. Brazil's term as a non-permanent Security Council member for the 1993–94 period and its claim to one of the permanent seats should the Council be enlarged might be linked to its renewed participation, but equally important has been the special responsibility it feels for UN operations in two Portuguese-speaking countries, Angola and Mozambique. In November 1994 total Brazilian staff in peacekeeping operations numbered 156,[46] over half of them in Angola and Mozambique.

From official statements, it is clear that Brazil considers present UN peacekeeping practices problematic, particularly the growing recourse to enforcement actions under Chapter VII. To correct this Brazil advocates principles which should govern UN operations and which would help confine mandates to traditional peacekeeping. It has also expressed concern about the blurring of objectives:

While in many cases peacekeeping operations are conducted in support of humanitarian and development assistance programmes, we should be cautious to not confuse their respective mandates and objectives. Besides the conceptual difficulties involved, the integration of the humanitarian component in the peacekeeping operations, as important as it might be in some instances, can multiply the logistics and planning problems of all too often over-stretched missions.[47]

---

[45] From 1956 to 1967 a total of 6300 Brazilian troops were deployed in Suez as part of UNEF I. Brazil also participated during 1960–64 in the UN operation in the Congo.

[46] 'United Nations peace-keeping' (note 3).

[47] Statement by Minister Edgard Telles Ribeiro to the Fourth Committee of the General Assembly on agenda item 87, 'Comprehensive review of the whole question of peace-keeping operations in all their aspects', New York, 29 Nov. 1993 (note 43).

Brazil considers peacekeeping operations a 'valuable conflict management technique', but rightly believes that they do not 'by themselves constitute a full-fledged security system'.[48] Brazil would like to see more 'preventive peacekeeping' and more emphasis by the UN on economic and social development. It has often expressed dismay that a country apparently needs to go through conflict and war before being considered ripe for 'peace building'—that is, assistance with economic and social reconstruction. Despite these doubts Brazil has affirmed that it is 'working with a view to increasing substantially' its participation in peacekeeping. A major difficulty is the need to obtain parliamentary approval for troop participation, a process that can take up to a year. This explains why Brazil's deployments have until relatively recently been limited to military observers. Efforts to streamline the approval process are reportedly under way.

Brazil's efforts to increase its participation significantly are as yet untested. Public opinion is more concerned with domestic socioeconomic problems and support for the government to increase its commitments abroad is only beginning to emerge. A February 1994 article by Brazil's Permanent Representative to the UN entitled 'Hard times for the United Nations' aimed to raise domestic awareness of UN issues. While it was critical of aspects of the UN, particularly of the Security Council, it concluded that:

Brazil has done its part. It has fully performed the multilateral role that is expected from the semi-continental size of the country, from the talents and work of its population, from its regional significance, from the tradition of its foreign policy and from its adherence to the great causes of democracy, socio-economic development and human rights.[49]

VII. Africa: a continent in need of peacekeepers

Although African nations have a tradition of providing troops to the UN, the instability of African countries has recently made this continent the largest recipient of UN peacekeeping troops. UN forces are at present deployed in Angola, Liberia, Mozambique, Rwanda, Uganda

---

[48] Statement by Ambassador Henrique R. Valle to the UN Special Committee on Peace-keeping Operations, New York, 31 Mar. 199. Unpublished.
[49] Sardenberg, R. M., 'Tempos difíceis para as Nações Unidas' [Hard times for the United Nations], *O Estado de São Paulo, Caderno 1, Espaço aberto São Paulo*, 4 Feb. 1994, p. A2 (in Portuguese).

and Western Sahara. While Ghana, Kenya, Nigeria, Senegal and Tunisia have been traditional troop contributors for years, there have been few newcomers. Egypt, Morocco, Namibia and Zimbabwe have recently come forward.

Morocco

Morocco's motivation may be linked to its membership of the Security Council in 1992–93 and to its desire to improve its standing in the international community which has been tarnished by its efforts to obtain control of Western Sahara and to tilt the political and military balance there in its favour. Morocco had 1382 troops in Somalia and civilian police in UNTAC, but, despite Africa's increasing need for troops, no major offers have been made.[50] One of Morocco's problems has been the UN's handling of peacekeeping operations:

We wish to stress the need for the Security Council and the UN Secretariat to incorporate in their approach an in-depth analysis of the socio-cultural component of the intended intervention zone . . . ignorance or misunderstanding of the human dimension could delay the establishment of a just and lasting peace, and would thus prove costly to the Organization in human and financial terms.[51]

Morocco has welcomed the Secretary-General's recommendations about peacemaking and peacekeeping but considers it 'imperative' to clarify these concepts, believing that a consensus genuinely reflecting the concerns of all members of the international community does not yet exist. Concerning the human rights component in UN operations, for example, Morocco has pointed out that 'the political dimension of human rights should not prevail over the social and economic one, which covers the basic needs of man including food, clothing, health care and shelter'.[52] This does not augur well for future contributions from Morocco, and UNOSOM II and UNTAC might remain isolated examples.

[50] On 30 Nov. 1994, 2 civilian policemen from Morocco were involved in UNAVEM II. See 'United Nations peace-keeping' (note 3).

[51] Statement by Abdelhakim el Amrani to the Fourth Committee of the General Assembly on agenda item 87, 'Comprehensive review of the whole question of peace-keeping operations in all their aspects', New York, 30 Nov. 1993 (note 40).

[52] Address by Foreign Minister Abdellatif Filali to the UN General Assembly, New York, 27 Sep. 1993, UN document A/48/PV.4.

Zimbabwe

Zimbabwe's main contribution has also been to UNOSOM II (994 soldiers),[53] but a handful of military observers have also been sent to three other African UN operations.[54] President Robert Mugabe's address to the UN General Assembly in 1993 underlined Zimbabwe's commitment to the African continent and argued in favour of UN cooperation with regional organizations, particularly the Organization of African Unity (OAU). While challenging Western domination of the Security Council and urging reform of the system to allow for more participation and transparency, President Mugabe nevertheless stated:

As equal members of this family of nations, we believe that peacekeeping, peace-building and peacemaking must not be the preserve of a few economically or politically powerful countries. We stand ready to cooperate with the international community in seeking solutions to the many problems facing the world today, by participating in peacekeeping operations or mediation efforts, or by providing any facilities or expertise at our disposal. However, unless all member states commit themselves to timely payments of their assessed contributions for these efforts, some countries will find continued participation difficult.[55]

Zimbabwe's contribution must be seen against the background of its late attainment of statehood, roughly 20 years after most other African countries. Hence it has focused from the beginning on a strong commitment to the total liberation of the African continent. Zimbabwe held the chairmanship of the NAM in 1985–88 and has been a positive, integrating force in the OAU. Its move into the UN arena and participation in UN peacekeeping operations, albeit with a regional emphasis, is therefore a logical progression and will probably continue.

Egypt

The most prominent African country to have recently joined the ranks of major contributors is Egypt, which in the latter half of 1993 alone

---

[53] 'United Nations peace-keeping' (note 3).
[54] UNAVEM II, UNAMIR and UNOMUR.
[55] Address by President Robert Mugabe to the UN General Assembly, New York, 28 Sep. 1993, UN document A/48/PV.7.

doubled its participation, mostly in Somalia and Bosnia and Herzegovina. As of 31 December 1993, Egypt had 2200 UN personnel in Somalia (1711), Bosnia and Herzegovina (446), Mozambique (20), Liberia (15) and Western Sahara (8).

Several factors can account for this change. First, the settlement of the Arab–Israeli conflict eliminated a major preoccupation and allowed Egypt to focus on other, external issues. Second, Egypt has a strong sense of political responsibility, anchored in history, of which its concern over the situation in Somalia, for example, is proof. It was a founding member not only of the UN but also of the OAU, the League of Arab States and the Organization of the Islamic Conference. Helping other African nations is a matter of obligation, prestige and pride. Egypt also considers it its duty to come to the assistance of other Muslim nations, which explains why the majority of its forces were sent to Bosnia and Herzegovina and Somalia. Its increased participation can also be attributed to the UN Secretary-General's personal intercession with President Hosni Mubarak to provide Egyptian troops at short notice. As no parliamentary approval is needed, the president, in consultation with the minister of defence, can quickly decide on each deployment.

One reason is undoubtedly financial. The economic situation in Egypt has deteriorated to such an extent that the government is hard pressed to provide the armed forces with their accustomed standard of living. The monthly reimbursement by the UN of some $1000 per soldier per month is princely in a country with an average annual per capita income of $610. UN assignments are therefore highly coveted and officers are known to have volunteered for lower-rank assignments in order to be eligible for UN duty. The actual financial rewards have been meagre so far, however, since payments from the UN have been slow and disputes have developed over the reimbursement rate for 'contingent-owned equipment'. In mid-1994 Egypt was owed $4.6 million by the UN for troop costs alone and has threatened to withdraw its forces if the arrears are not paid.[56] It has been vocifer-

---

[56] Troop costs are, in fact, the tip of the iceberg and only amounted to a total of $334.8 million which the UN owes to 61 member states (as of 31 Dec. 1993). Reimbursements for 'contingent-owned equipment' account for the greater part. Egypt, for example, claims from the UN $103 million for equipment used by its troops in Somalia and the former Yugoslavia. While a country like Egypt can ill afford such arrears, even relatively prosperous Singapore has repeatedly complained about the outstanding reimbursement of $1 million for medical helicopters provided to UNTAC.

ous in criticizing Western countries for not paying their peacekeeping assessments on time.[57]

As a heavily militarized country where the government is in control 'at the sufferance of the army', as one diplomatic observer put it, sending troops abroad at a time when there is no external threat helps Egypt to prevent military unrest and keep its government in power. Moreover there is general approval of the government's peacekeeping policy. The presence of Egyptian troops in Somalia was a matter of national pride and referred to in the press as 'a situation that does us honour'.[58] The death of an Egyptian soldier in Somalia was seen as the necessary price to be paid for such engagements.

The most powerful motivation for Egypt's involvement may be its aspiration to be a major international player:

Egypt—which is undertaking an effective role within the international order in the formulation of regional and international relations and in establishing the concepts and principles on which we all agree, in addition to its participation in numerous peacekeeping operations on several continents—has the right and the potential to contribute to the proposed restructuring of the United Nations. Egypt has the desire and determination to take part in both the process itself and in setting the standards and values to be used in the process. Egypt believes that it has now gained the requisite standing to be included within the framework of the ongoing discussion and within the new membership.[59]

Egypt will undoubtedly use its participation in UN peacekeeping operations to continue to press its claims for higher standing in the international community.

VIII. Conclusion

As the above cases show, domestic considerations are the prime factor motivating a country to contribute or not to contribute troops to UN peacekeeping operations. While pressure from a major outside power or within a security alliance may occasionally tilt the balance, this is

[57] As of 31 Jan. 1994 the UN was owed $2.7 billion by member states, of which $1.4 billion was for peacekeeping. The total peacekeeping bill for 1993 amounted to $3 billion.
[58] *al-Ahram*, 15 Feb. 1994, p. 1 and 16 Feb. 1994, p. 1.
[59] Foreign Minister Amre Moussa, Address to the UN General Assembly, New York, 27 Sep. 1993, UN document A/48/PV.5.

clearly of less consequence. International ambitions, regional security, ideological or religious factors and economic interests are paramount.

A rapid increase in the number of casualties suffered by UN troops has affected troop availability. It is harder for governments to defend the deaths of their soldiers on distant battlefields. The 'noble cause' of peacekeeping has received some dents in the former Yugoslavia and Somalia. Moreover, a large number of states do not subscribe to the current peacekeeping philosophy and practice, as an examination of the above countries has shown. Some nevertheless contribute troops while waiting for a new consensus to emerge, while others, out of principle, do not. The expansion of mandates and new tasks given to UN operations have added to the difficulties of recruiting new peace-keepers.

Among the remedies currently being discussed—providing better training and equipment, encouraging the establishment of additional national (or regional) peacekeeping training centres—the most prom-ising is national stand-by arrangements, first proposed by President François Mitterrand of France and endorsed by the Secretary-General in his 1992 *Agenda for Peace*.[60] While this would undoubtedly speed up deployment of UN forces, ultimately the total number of UN peacekeeping troops in the field will fall. The quagmires of the former Yugoslavia and Somalia have made the international community cau-tious. No large-scale UN operations are being considered at present, although the situation in several countries could qualify for inter-vention on a massive scale. Which will the international community take up?

---

[60] UN, An Agenda for Peace: Preventive Diplomacy, Peacemaking and Peacekeeping, Report of the Secretary-General, UN document A/47/277, S/24111, 17 June 1992.

7. The Organization for Security and Co-operation in Europe

Jerzy M. Nowak*

I. A glance at the recent past

Like other international bodies, the CSCE—from January 1995 the OSCE[1]—faced the new post-cold war risks, challenges and unconventional situations unprepared. It had no concepts, instruments or structures to deal with the post-communist transformation: the disintegration of the bipolar East–West system, the collapse of the Soviet Union, the explosion of nationalist fervour, large-scale violations of human rights, local conflicts rooted in ethnic and religious animosities, regional wars and other dangers.

Before 1989 the CSCE process managed partially to alleviate the burdens of the East–West divide, open channels of communication, contribute to military security and establish norms of cooperation between states. It also developed the important concept that a state's internal actions are the legitimate business of other nations if they affect political freedom and human rights. The historic changes of 1989 exhausted its traditional agenda of the mid-1970s and from then on the CSCE searched for a new identity. While maintaining its basic values and procedures, it turned mainly to preventive diplomacy and crisis and conflict management and resolution.

The Charter of Paris for a New Europe of November 1990 embodied expectations of an increased CSCE role in solving European problems in the new depolarized system. However, the euphoria that followed the 1989 'autumn of the peoples' did not favour rational analysis of the looming threats and risks. Hence the Charter of Paris and its Supplementary Document did not even refer to peacekeeping.[2]

---

[1] Here called the CSCE for the period up to the end of 1994 and OSCE from 1 Jan. 1995.

[2] Many of the CSCE documents referred to are reproduced in Bloed, A. (ed.), *The Conference on Security and Co-operation in Europe: Analysis and Basic Documents, 1972–1993* (Kluwer Academic Publishers: Dordrecht, 1993). The Charter of Paris is reproduced in *SIPRI Yearbook 1991: World Armaments and Disarmament* (Oxford University Press: Oxford, 1991), pp. 603–10.

* This chapter represents the personal views of the author and not those of his government.

However, it did formulate a mandate allowing some forms of external *droit de regard* over internal affairs in respect of human rights. It also inaugurated CSCE structures which in time would begin to respond to the new challenges. This was the first indication that the CSCE was changing from a forum for dialogue and negotiation to an operational structure.

Of all the international bodies the CSCE has changed most in the post-cold war period in response to the pressures of the new era. It has ceased to be the 'Helsinki process', a discussion club or a nascent international organization and has been transformed into a regional security arrangement as defined in Chapter VII of the UN Charter, based on well-defined common values and political obligations.[3] By declaring itself a regional arrangement, the CSCE established a link not only with the UN as an institution but also between the European and global security systems.

The conflict prevention and peacekeeping ethos of what is now the OSCE is based on cooperation, persuasion and a painstaking search for consensus. These characteristics are simultaneously its strength and its weakness—strength, because consultation and consensus building allow it to mobilize the whole of the OSCE community, including the parties in conflict, to cooperate in applying democratic standards, to focus on the root causes of problems and to seek common solutions to conflicts; weakness, because the OSCE process is slow as it tries to persuade parties to cooperate instead of punishing violations of agreed standards or attempting to enforce the peace. This distinguishes the OSCE's approach from that of the UN. The OSCE is, however, still in search of its own niche in international efforts aimed at conflict prevention, management and resolution, including peacekeeping. Peacekeeping should be seen as an integral part of its overall concept of the management of change.[4] Traditional UN-style peacekeeping is at present not at the forefront of OSCE actions but is in the planning stages and may yet assume significance.

---

[3] Rotfeld, A. D., 'The CSCE: towards a security organization', *SIPRI Yearbook 1993: World Armaments and Disarmament* (Oxford University Press: Oxford, 1993), pp. 171–89; and Szafarz, R., 'CSCE: an international organization *in statu nascendi?*', *Legal Aspects of a New European Infrastructure* (Netherlands Helsinki Committee: Utrecht, 1992), pp. 15–21.

[4] 'The CSCE and the management of change' from the Helsinki Summit Declaration of July 1992, part of the Helsinki Document 1992. See 'CSCE, Helsinki Document 1992: The Challenges of Change', ed. Bloed (note 2), pp. 18–47; and excerpts published in *SIPRI Yearbook 1993* (note 3), pp. 190–209.

II. OSCE instruments for conflict prevention, management and resolution

Early warning and conflict prevention

In accordance with the CSCE Helsinki Document of 10 July 1992,[5] the CSCE and now the OSCE have experimented with various instruments for early warning and conflict prevention. Five are identifiable, and the first three are of particular importance:

1. A system of intensive and regular political consultations and dialogue on security challenges and conflict prevention has been created, centred now on the Permanent Council in Vienna, the OSCE's first permanent body for political consultation and decision making. Early warning instruments also include regular implementation debates (in particular on human rights), confidence- and security-building measures (CSBMs) and the work of the Office for Democratic Institutions and Human Rights (ODIHR) in Warsaw, which has become a real conflict prevention instrument in the OSCE human dimension.

2. 'Mechanisms' have been devised to mobilize concerted action. In the military field these include the Vienna Mechanism on unusual military activities and the mechanism for discussion and clarification of hazardous military incidents.[6] In the human dimension they consist of the Moscow Mechanism with its set of obligatory procedures for examining human rights violations, including bilateral meetings, the provision of information and invitation of an OSCE mission of experts.[7] In the political field an example is the Berlin Mechanism, also obligatory, which provides for requests for clarification, information and meetings at short notice in emergency situations.[8] Unfortunately they have been little used. In March 1994 the CSCE Permanent Committee began discussions on ways of improving their effectiveness and these initial discussions made some progress towards consolidating the existing mechanisms, making their use obligatory in

[5] See note 4.

[6] Established by the Vienna Document 1990 on Confidence- and Security-Building Measures, section II (Risk Reduction), paras 17 and 18. See *SIPRI Yearbook 1991* (note 2), pp. 477–78.

[7] Document of the Moscow Meeting of the Conference on the Human Dimension of the CSCE, Moscow, 3 Oct. 1991, para. 2,

[8] CSCE, First Meeting of the CSCE Council, 19–20 June 1991, Summary of conclusions, Annex 2, Mechanism for consultation and co-operation with regard to emergency situation, CSCE document [CSCE, 20 June 1991].

a wider range of circumstances and enhancing awareness of the potential of the mechanisms. By mid-1995, however, concrete steps had still not been taken.

3. A High Commissioner on National Minorities (HCNM) was appointed as an instrument for conflict prevention at the earliest stage, to provide early warning and propose early action.[9]

A successful record has been achieved through the discreet diplomacy of Max van der Stoel, in particular in the Baltic states, Albania, Hungary, Macedonia and Slovakia. His activities in the CIS have concentrated on Kazakhstan, Kyrgyzstan and Ukraine (Crimea). In his work he has gone beyond early warning to an early containment phase in response to political needs in the field.[10]

4. Legal instruments for the peaceful settlement of disputes have been developed, including the Convention on Conciliation and Arbitration, signed by 33 states (which had not yet entered into force in mid-1995)[11] and a mechanism for the peaceful settlement of disputes. The latter, known as the Valletta Procedure or Mechanism, envisages a third-party function to reconcile differing positions and prevent disputes from escalating.[12]

None of these instruments has been used so far, since they are probably considered by the interested parties as excessively intrusive and likely to formally highlight a conflict instead of allowing resort to more discreet and subtle action. They are periodically critically reviewed for their effectiveness and utility.

5. New 'stabilizing measures' of a military nature for application in localized crisis situations were agreed by the CSCE's Forum for Security Co-operation (FSC) in November 1993.[13] They comprise a list of voluntary stabilizing measures intended to facilitate decision making and the search for specific, short-term measures in support of

[9] CSCE, Helsinki Document 1992 (note 6), Helsinki Decisions, section 23. On the first stage of the High Commissioner's activities, see CSCE, Office of the Secretary General, *Annual Report 1993 on CSCE Activities*, 30 Nov. 1993, pp. 10–11.

[10] van der Stoel, M., 'Preventing conflict and building peace: a challenge for the CSCE', *NATO Review*, no. 4 (1994), p. 16.

[11] 'CSCE, Decisions of Stockholm Council Meeting (14–15 Dec. 1992), Convention on Conciliation and Arbitration within the CSCE', ed. Bloed (note 2), pp. 870–99.

[12] 'CSCE, Report of the CSCE Meeting of Experts on Peaceful Settlement of Disputes, Valletta, 8 Feb. 1991', ed. Bloed (note 2), pp. 567–81; and 'Modification to section V of the Valletta Procedure in the Stockholm Council Meeting Decisions', ed. Bloed (note 2), p. 689.

[13] CSCE, 49th Plenary Meeting of the Special Committee of the CSCE Forum for Security Co-operation, Vienna, 24 Nov.–1 Dec. 1993, 'Stabilizing measures for localized crisis situations', *FSC Journal,* 24 Nov. 1993, no. 49, Annex 2.

a political reconciliation process. They range from various forms of military information exchange, through local demilitarization, to on-site verification and monitoring.

Among the above instruments the most successful and effective to date have been the consultation system, which permits constructive 'internationalization' of a problem, and two institutions—the HCNM and the ODIHR.

Conflict management

The OSCE conflict management concept has been developed progressively and pragmatically. The available instruments and modalities have been adjusted to the emerging challenges.

Overall responsibility for applying crisis management instruments rests with the OSCE's political bodies, in particular the Chairman-in-Office (CIO), aided where necessary by the previous and next chairmen working together as the 'Troika' and by the Senior Council and Permanent Council. They consider possible or actual conflicts, initiate courses of action and supervise them. The Secretariat has been operational since September 1993 and has been increasing its role in support of crisis management. The functions of the Conflict Prevention Centre (CPC) have never quite corresponded to its name, as it deals mainly with OSCE peace mission support and the functioning of the CSBM regime.

To date the OSCE has dealt with conflict situations in Estonia, Georgia, Latvia, Moldova, Nagorno-Karabakh, the Russian Federation (Chechnya), Tajikistan, Ukraine (Crimea) and the former Yugoslavia. Participation of the parties to the conflict in the OSCE efforts is an important feature. The objective is to establish a permanent framework for conflict management and resolution and to assist the parties to conduct a dialogue. Three types of activity have been undertaken.

1. *Ad hoc* steering groups have been created to deal with specific conflicts. The Minsk Group,[14] set up to mediate and attempt to settle the conflict in Nagorno-Karabakh, is one example.

[14] Set up in Mar. 1992 and originally consisting of Armenia and Azerbaijan (the parties to the conflict), Czechoslovakia, Italy and Sweden (the 3 members of the CSCE Troika at the time the Group was set up), Belarus, France, Germany, Russia, Turkey and the USA.

2. Personal representatives of the CIO and OSCE peace missions have been dispatched to the field to offer their good offices, monitor situations, help avert political conflicts, mainly of an internal nature, and assist in democracy-building. By mid-1995 nine such missions and one 'Assistance Group' (in Grozny) had been established.

In the former Yugoslavia the OSCE has taken the lead in defining humanitarian standards that must apply even in situations of conflict. The objectives of the missions of long duration to Kosovo, Sanjak and Vojvodina (August 1992–July 1993) included *inter alia* monitoring violations of human rights and providing the local population with a kind of ombudsman service.[15] In June 1994 the mission in Sarajevo was established. Its main purpose is to support the ombudsmen appointed by the OSCE after consultation with the President and Vice-President of Bosnia and Herzegovina. They remain in contact with international and non-governmental organizations and report to the OSCE on matters pertaining to the human dimension of the conflict. An innovative step was taken when the Spillover Monitor Mission to Skopje was deployed in September 1992 to prevent a spill-over of the conflict to other parts of the former Yugoslavia. It includes military observers and cooperates with UNPREDEP, the Macedonia Command of UNPROFOR. The Sanctions Assistance Missions, with field support from the WEU, have provided innovative operational experience approximating to preventive diplomacy.

In the newly independent states of the former Soviet Union missions have been established in Estonia, Georgia, Latvia, Moldova and Tajikistan.

The Mission to Georgia was installed in Tbilisi on 3 December 1992. The mandate envisaged initiation of discussions with the leadership of the self-proclaimed Republic of South Ossetia, liaison with local military commanders in support of the existing cease-fire, the gathering of information on the military situation and the investigation of violent incidents. It also envisaged that the mission would seek to work out a negotiating framework for the Abkhazian conflict, but the lead role in this case was assumed by the UN, which showed no interest in OSCE involvement. In March 1994 a new mandate for the Mission to Georgia was established, including monitoring of the joint

---

Slovakia succeeded Czechoslovakia and was then replaced by Hungary in Dec. 1993; Switzerland was added in Dec. 1994 and Finland in Apr. 1995. See also section IV of this chapter.

[15] The mission was withdrawn on the insistence of Belgrade in July 1993 but continues to operate formally from Vienna as an open-ended ad hoc group which shares information.

peacekeeping forces, composed mainly of Russian contingents, established by the Sochi Agreement of 24 June 1992. This created the precedent of a certain form of cooperation with a third party in a conflict, in this case the CIS.

In April 1993 a mission was deployed in Moldova to help achieve a comprehensive political settlement to the conflict in Trans-Dniester. It established contacts with the Moldovan Government in Cisinau and with the Trans-Dniester leadership in Tiraspol. The CSCE mission to Tajikistan was installed in Dushanbe in February 1994 with the main task of facilitating dialogue and confidence building between the government and the Islamic opposition. Two small-scale missions to Estonia (December 1992) and Latvia (September 1993) were aimed at helping these nations to rebuild their civil societies and develop a dialogue with their Russian-speaking communities. Their activities embraced *inter alia* citizenship issues, legislation concerning aliens, local government elections and round tables as vehicles for national dialogue.[16] In August 1994 the CSCE sent a mission to Ukraine to facilitate dialogue between the central government and the Crimean authorities concerning the autonomous status of the Republic of Crimea within Ukraine. Finally, in April 1995 the OSCE sent an Assistance Group to Chechnya to 'promote the peaceful resolution of the crisis and the stabilization in the Chechen republic'.[17]

3. The OSCE has legitimized or given support to action undertaken by other international organizations. It endorsed small but innovative operations like the deployment of the European Community (EC) Monitoring Mission to the former Yugoslavia and 'welcomed' the establishment of a military patrol operation on the Danube by the WEU to monitor sanctions compliance, thereby according the mission greater legitimacy.

4. The OSCE may establish its own peacekeeping operations. It and the UN are the only bodies in Europe vested with the power to conduct peacekeeping, although in the OSCE's case without enforcement

---

[16] A round table was established by the President of Estonia in July 1993; the CSCE mission played an active part in the drafting of its statute and as a legal adviser.

[17] On missions and their mandates, see OSCE, Conflict Prevention Centre, Survey of OSCE long-term missions, local OSCE representatives and Sanctions Assistance Missions, OSCE document REF.SEC/64/95, 15 May 1995; Rotfeld, A. D., 'Europe: the multilateral security process', *SIPRI Yearbook 1995: Armaments, Disarmament and International Security* (Oxford University Press: Oxford, 1995), pp. 290–94; and Carlsson, S. (ed.), *The Challenge of Preventive Diplomacy: the Experience of the CSCE* (Ministry for Foreign Affairs: Stockholm, 1994).

action. Chapter III of the 1992 Helsinki Decisions set politically binding commitments by which participating states declared that peacekeeping activities are politically possible and legitimate as an instrument for conflict prevention and crisis management. In the absence of UN Security Council authorization, the OSCE would need the consent of the state on whose territory such an operation was to be conducted.

These diversified activities are the result of a pragmatic approach by the OSCE to the management of conflicts. The mandates and modalities of such peace missions are slowly producing OSCE doctrine in this field, part of which relates to peacekeeping.

III. The OSCE's peacekeeping doctrine

The intellectual and political origins of OSCE peacekeeping may be found in the Charter of Paris of 1990 and its idea of 'common efforts in the field of military security'. However, the Charter did not develop this idea. The term 'peacekeeping' appeared for the first time in CSCE vocabulary in the Prague Document on Further Development of CSCE Institutions and Structures adopted by the Council in Prague in January 1992. The Council asked the Helsinki Follow-up Meeting 'to give careful consideration to possibilities for CSCE peacekeeping or a CSCE role in peacekeeping'.[18]

The discussions that followed in Vienna revealed that a number of states were in favour of undertaking traditional peacekeeping missions based on military participation within the CSCE framework. Others argued that the CSCE had very limited organizational capacity to embark on such an endeavour. They were even opposed to the idea of creating middle-sized monitoring missions of up to 500 members with a mandate to observe and monitor a cease-fire. Their conclusion was that larger military operations would require considerable investment in equipment, logistics, communication and transport, which could be arranged only through cooperation with NATO or the WEU. They also argued that the CSCE was unprepared for any major financial or material commitment in this respect. They preferred small-scale missions centred on conflict prevention. This view prevailed.

It was interesting that the division of views did not initially run along the usual line—between NATO members and other states. The

[18] Bloed (note 2), p. 834.

only proposal tabled at the Helsinki Follow-up Meeting which had the term 'peacekeeping' in its title was submitted by a group of 14 countries on 6 April 1992.[19] A second, more cautious, proposal was put forward as late as 3 June 1992 by Portugal on behalf of the EC.[20] It was also clear that the USA, which sponsored neither proposal, was sceptical about the CSCE's capabilities and favoured authorization for the CSCE to use NATO whenever necessary.

The Helsinki Summit Declaration stated that the participating states 'have provided for CSCE peacekeeping according to agreed modalities'. This was an overstatement. Not much in fact was provided in real terms except a set of rules, some of which were to be developed further in Vienna. Its importance, however, rested in its declaration of CSCE peacekeeping activities as possible and politically legitimate.

Chapter III of the Helsinki Decisions of 1992 was devoted to 'Early warning, conflict prevention and crisis management (including factfinding and rapporteur missions and CSCE peacekeeping), [and] peaceful settlement of disputes'. The subsection on CSCE peacekeeping began with another overstatement: 'Peacekeeping constitutes an important operational element of the overall capability of the CSCE for conflict prevention and crisis management intended to complement the political process of dispute resolution'.[21] This should be seen as a declaration of intent rather than as a description of reality. There was and continues to be a limited OSCE capability for conflict prevention, and only a potential for peacekeeping as the term is understood by the UN. However, an important step forward had been taken, allowing later preparations for a peacekeeping operation in Nagorno-Karabakh to begin.[22]

The same subsection contained a detailed description of what a CSCE operation might look like and provided a general mandate for peacekeeping activities in cases of conflict within or between participating states. Depending on the political and military situation in the mission area, such operations may comprise civilian and/or military components, assuming a variety of forms, from observer and moni-

---

[19] Austria, Canada, the Czech and Slovak Federal Republic, Denmark, Estonia, Finland, Hungary, Iceland, Norway, Poland, Slovenia, Sweden, Switzerland and Ukraine. See CSCE, Helsinki Follow-up Meeting, Peacekeeping under the auspices of the CSCE: an outline, CSCE document CSCE/HM/WG.1, 6 Apr. 1992 (mimeographed).

[20] CSCE, Helsinki Follow-up Meeting, Conflict prevention, crisis management and dispute resolution, CSCE document CSCE/HM/WG.1/9/Rev. 1, 3 June 1992.

[21] CSCE, Helsinki Document 1992 (note 4), Helsinki Decisions, sections III, 17–56.

[22] See section V below.

toring missions to a larger deployment of forces, including battalion size. Possible aims include: (*a*) supervision and assistance in monitoring cease-fires; (*b*) monitoring of troop withdrawals; (*c*) support for the maintainance of law and order; (*d*) assistance in building civil society, the settlement of conflicts with national and other minorities and the establishment of a system of political and military CSBMs; and (*e*) provision of humanitarian and medical aid and assistance for refugees. None of these tasks should entail enforcement action, which is reserved only for forces authorized by the UN Security Council, but this restriction might be circumvented through bilateral cooperation between the two organizations.

The Helsinki Decisions contained a number of self-imposed limitations, for instance on tasks (the exclusion of peace enforcement), the size of operations and decision-making processes (the prerogatives of the UN Security Council were acknowledged). They also included some preconditions such as the consent of 'all parties concerned', the existence of a 'durable' cease-fire and a consensus decision by the CSCE Council or the Committee of Senior Officials (from 1995 the Senior Council). The Helsinki Decisions also dealt with a number of detailed questions like chain of command, appointment of head of mission, financial arrangements and cooperation with regional and transatlantic organizations. In the latter case the Helsinki Document authorized the CSCE to request the EC, NATO and the WEU, on a case-by-case basis, to make their resources available in support of peacekeeping activities. The CIS was also mentioned explicitly as a 'mechanism' to be approached for possible support.

On the basis of these decisions, considerable preparations for peacekeeping have been made within the OSCE structures, but peacekeeping operations in the traditional sense of the word have not yet been initiated. At present what are commonly called OSCE peacekeeping operations are long-term missions on a smaller or larger scale, established to maintain favourable conditions for preventing conflicts from breaking out or spreading as well as for facilitating negotiations. Some have military officers on their staff. The Helsinki Decisions regarding peacekeeping have so far mainly been used in organizing and running these missions. The decisions on peacekeeping have been made but await implementation. Preparatory work has continued.

IV. The OSCE conflict management and peacekeeping infrastructure

Peacekeeping operations or peace missions may be initiated by the OSCE following a request by one or more participating states to the CIO, Senior Council or Permanent Council. The Permanent Council, a body permanently in session, is the main forum for consultations concerning conflict management. It finalizes mandates for the missions, scrutinizes their day-to-day activities, reviews them regularly and takes the necessary decisions on their conduct.

Decisions on peacekeeping operations require consensus and can be taken only when all parties concerned have demonstrated their commitment to creating favourable conditions for the operations and their willingness to cooperate. This cooperative method is more effective as it involves all interested parties, including the parties to the conflict, but produces a relatively long decision-making process, especially in cases of intra-state conflicts. In Nagorno-Karabakh the refusal of the parties to consent to a peacekeeping operation continues to be the main stumbling-block.

The CIO is responsible for initiating political consultations with the parties concerned and does not require a consensus of the participating states to do this. The CIO may be assisted by the Troika, informal steering groups established on a case-by-case basis, and personal representatives designated by the CIO to provide support, in particular in the initial phase. Promising experience has been gained with the use of personal representatives of the CIO who, assisted by political and military experts, may be sent to the area of conflict to assess the possibilities for further engagement of the OSCE. The detailed tasks of the personal representative include negotiations on the necessary memoranda of understanding with the parties concerned and reconnaissance of the political and military situation in the area, giving special attention to the establishment and observance of an effective and durable cease-fire and the prospects for a comprehensive political solution. Personal representatives such as Adam Daniel Rotfeld (Poland) in Moldova, Mathias Mossberg and Jan Eliasson (Sweden) in Nagorno-Karabakh, Istvan Gyarmati (Hungary) in Georgia and Chechnya and Olivier Roy (France) in Tajikistan have contributed substantially to the OSCE conflict prevention and management processes. The reports of the personal representatives, together with the results of consultations within the Permanent Council, are usually the main basis for the decision to dispatch a long-term peace mission. Such a decision includes the adoption of a clear and precise mandate and modalities.

Operational support to missions in the field is rendered by the Section for Mission Support of the CPC, which provides logistical and administrative follow-up to recommendations and keeps open a 24-hour point of contact with the missions. The Head of Mission is nominated by and responsible to the CIO, to whom he is obliged to report. In practice, however, day-to-day reporting is to the Permanent Council. The Head of Mission has operational command in the mission area and may appoint his own deputy.

The mandate and terms of reference constitute the main basis for planning by the CPC. OCSE peace missions have so far been planned with great efficiency and cost-effectiveness and there is some satisfaction that its peacekeeping activities are not overburdened by bureaucracy or costly by UN standards, although UN operations are of course on a vastly greater scale and have not had the luxury of advance planning such as the OSCE has had.

The costs of the operations are borne by all OSCE participating states in accordance with the OSCE scale of contributions. Additional voluntary contributions by participating states are also welcomed. In some cases considerable financial and material support has been given, mainly by the USA, the European Union, the Nordic states and Japan (which has special status at the OSCE).[23]

The CPC has calculated the start-up costs for a hypothetical small-scale mission consisting of eight members deployed at one base office and three field posts for an initial period of three months. It is assumed that accommodation would be provided by the host government, local staff would be hired, and some office equipment would be available locally. On this basis, estimated costs amount to approximately $400 000 per year. However, the larger mission of long duration to Georgia, comprising 20 members, costs $2 million per year.

---

[23] According to the 1992 Helsinki Decisions, part IV, paras 9–11, Japan was invited to attend CSCE meetings, including those of heads of state and government, the CSCE Council, the Committee of Senior Officials (Senior Council) and other appropriate bodies which consider specific topics of expanded consultation and cooperation. The latter means in particular attendance at meetings of the Permanent Council and the FSC. Japan 'may contribute' to such meetings but cannot participate in the preparation and adoption of decisions.

V. Challenges for the OSCE peacekeepers

Nagorno-Karabakh

In 1994 the CSCE began feasibility studies for deployment of a multinational peacekeeping mission for the Nagorno-Karabakh conflict, which entered its armed phase in 1988 and intensified after the disintegration of the Soviet Union in 1991. In 1992, as a result of two rapporteur missions to the region in January and March of that year, the CSCE convened a conference on Nagorno-Karabakh in Minsk, whose participants became known as the Minsk Group.[24] The Minsk Conference and the Minsk Group set a precedent for the CSCE.

From the very beginning the difficulty was harmonizing CSCE efforts with those of the Russian Federation. This was solved formally by establishing co-chairmanships of the Minsk Conference and the Minsk Group.

On 12 May 1994 the parties reached agreement in Moscow on an informal cease-fire. This enabled the CSCE to start to explore the possibility of deploying a multinational peacekeeping force. In the Budapest Document of the CSCE Review Conference and summit meeting of December 1994 it was decided to establish a High Level Planning Group (HLPG) in Vienna to make recommendations on the size and characteristics of such a force, command and control arrangements, rules of engagement and arrangements with contributing states.[25] The decision was based on the assumption that the parties would request and accept an OSCE peacekeeping mission, establish at an early date an effective and durable cease-fire and confirm their willingness to implement an agreement prepared by the Minsk Conference on the cessation of armed conflict. The objectives of the mission would be: (*a*) to monitor the implementation by the parties of the agreement to end the conflict and to support political negotiations; (*b*) to support the cease-fire and cessation of hostilities; and (*c*) to support withdrawal of troops from occupied areas and create the conditions for refugees to return.

---

[24] See note 14.

[25] CSCE, Budapest Declaration, Budapest Decisions, chapter II [CSCE, Dec. 1994]. The HLPG, composed mainly of military experts, succeeded the Initial Operation Planning Group (IOPG) formed in May 1993 for the same purpose. It has done extensive planning and adjusted it to the results of the work done by the Minsk Group.

The HLPG study outlined specific tasks and organizational aspects for the mission. It envisaged a force structure of three infantry battalions, two or three independent infantry companies, observers and support and logistics units, totalling about 3000 personnel at a cost of roughly $100 million for six months. Five phases were envisaged, from pre-deployment to conclusion of the mission. While the tasks of the mission would probably not include the provision of humanitarian aid, it might be required to assist in the delivery of such aid. This would not entail enforcement action.[26]

The HLPG helped establish the scale of the endeavour in terms of numbers of personnel and requirements relating to safety, equipment, budget, procurement and short-notice deployment. This led to much behind-the-scenes criticism among OSCE participating states that the OSCE was not prepared for such a large-scale operation and that it would require *inter alia* the reconstruction and strengthening of the HLPG and the CPC Mission Support Section and a radical increase in the OSCE budget.[27] Preferences were voiced for NATO logistical, equipment and communication support, but there was no political agreement on this either in the OSCE or in NATO. Obtaining pledges of contributions for the operation was extremely difficult, particularly for personnel costs.

In spite of these doubts and difficulties preparations proceeded. The Special Representative of the CIO and field representatives were sent to the area of conflict in mid-1995. The Minsk Group intensified its peace efforts. The OSCE was by and large prepared on paper to launch the operation but it was understood that it would be considerably smaller, in terms of personnel, than initially planned.

The launching of the operation requires the consent of the parties to the conflict, Russia and other major powers. At the time of writing, this was still lacking, in particular that of the parties to the conflict. Deployment may therefore be postponed until the spring of 1996: severe winter conditions in the region make deployment in winter very unlikely. The fate of the operation is widely regarded as an important test for the credibility of the OSCE.

---

[26] OSCE document 341/95, corrected version REF.CIO/23/95 Corr. 1, 27 June 1995, known as the 'Mission Statement'.

[27] The entire budget of the OSCE in 1995 was only $34 million.

Possible 'third party' participation in OSCE peacekeeping

The CSCE and the OSCE have constantly favoured a coordinated approach to actions undertaken by other states or regional structures.

The OSCE's involvement in the settlement of conflicts on the territory of the former USSR has led to a new specific challenge, namely whether and how to meet the Russian Federation's demand for support for its 'peacekeeping operations', sometimes conducted under the aegis of the CIS but with limited participation by other CIS members, and conducted near Russia's borders. Russia has shown in Moldova and Tajikistan that it is willing to deploy its forces to ensure stability in its conflict-troubled border areas.[28] Some operations have in fact prevented bloodshed, but have also resulted in the freezing of the conflicts, as in the cases of Abkhazia, Moldova and Tajikistan.

Russian and/or CIS military operations, which are referred to by the interested parties as 'peacekeeping', differ from UN or possible OSCE peacekeeping operations. They may include various forms of enforcement which in practice is decided by only one partner, Russia. Since they are conducted by one state only or under the CIS umbrella, they cannot be regarded as fully impartial. Such engagements are not mandated by any international organization—the CIS has not yet been recognized by the UN as a regional security arrangement under Chapter VII of the UN Charter—and imply the maintenance of Russian influence and control. Other OSCE states understand Russia's concerns over stability in its border areas but view them strictly in terms of OSCE principles and recognize no special role, rights or status for any territory which could imply that it was partly exempted from the OSCE's system of commitments.

Since early 1993 Russia has repeatedly indicated an interest in some form of OSCE involvement in its peacekeeping operations, and particularly in some form of political legitimization and financial support. From the beginning Russia has hinted that the political and material aspects of support were perhaps more important than legitimization. A request along those lines was made in November 1993 in Vienna.[29]

---

[28] Shustov, V., 'Peacekeeping in the CSCE: the Russian view', *Helsinki Monitor*, vol. 5, no. 2 (1994), pp. 7–10. This article also includes basic data reflecting the participation of Russian military personnel in peacekeeping operations in the conflict zones.

[29] Informal proposal by the delegation of the Russian Federation, 'On interaction between the CSCE and peacekeeping forces of the Russian Federation and CIS (provisions to be included into the Rome Communiqué)', Vienna, 5 Nov. 1993 (mimeographed).

Judging from its statements in the OSCE and the UN, Russia may be considering two approaches: (*a*) unilateral—peacekeeping within its own borders and in some former Soviet republics by Russia itself and at its own discretion; and (*b*) multilateral—ceding some responsibility to CIS countries or to other states under UN or OSCE authorization. It seems that priority is being given to the CIS, where Russia plays a leading role, and to the UN where Russia has a stronger position in decision making. This has led to further demands for a UN or OSCE mandate for Russia to conduct peacekeeping operations on the territory of the former Soviet Union, for international support for such operations, and for recognition of the CIS as a partner in peacekeeping operations on an equal footing with the UN, the OSCE or NATO. Furthermore, peacekeeping in the 'post-Soviet' space has often been linked to safeguarding the rights of the 'Russian-speaking population', a term which has been used to include not only Russians but other ethnic groups such as Belarussians and Ukrainians.

For other OSCE participating states, the Central and East European states in particular, this problem demands a proper balance between the requirements of stability and the strengthening of the independence and sovereignty of the newly independent states. It is in the interest of the OSCE states that a Russian stabilizing and peacekeeping role should be approved only on the basis of UN and OSCE principles, with control being exercised by international institutions and interventions being based on the freely expressed agreement of interested states. Acceptance of a Russian role should also be conditional on democratic domestic developments in Russia, especially the strengthening of civil control over the military. Some states, in particular the Baltic countries and Ukraine, view this problem in the larger context of the globalization of Russia's national interests and of possible recognition of a role for Russia as the guarantor of peace and stability within the post-Soviet space.

On the other hand Russia has demonstrated that it is able to deploy forces on the ground and that without its participation there is little prospect of stability on most of the territory of the former USSR. No other state has shown a willingness to send peacekeeping troops to these trouble-spots. It has therefore been generally recognized that it is in the interests of the international community to cooperate with Russia in this matter, but on specific conditions: (*a*) that the OSCE should be used as a forum for consultation before the initiation of any

Russian or CIS mission; (b) that the premises underlying such missions should be based on the principles of international law and OSCE norms of behaviour, in particular respect for the sovereignty of states; and (c) that the OSCE should take on the political monitoring or control of Russian and/or CIS missions and their operations.[30]

The Rome Council Meeting of the CSCE in December 1993 decided that 'exceptionally, on a case-by-case basis and under specific conditions, the CSCE may consider setting up a co-operative arrangement in order, *inter alia*, to ensure that the role and functions of the third-party military force in a conflict area are consistent with CSCE principles and objectives'.[31] The same decision also contained criteria that such a cooperative arrangement would require: respect for sovereignty and territorial integrity, the consent of the parties involved, impartiality, multinational character, a clear mandate, transparency and above all an integral link to a political process and a plan for orderly withdrawal. The Council called for further work on this issue.

Further efforts in the form of informal negotiations between the Russian Federation and the other CSCE states failed to produce agreement, mainly because Russia rejected the need for any international legitimization of Russian and CIS peacekeeping operations and insisted on the 'proportionality' principle. This meant that the degree of involvement of OSCE monitoring missions in these Russian or CIS operations was to be commensurate with their 'political, financial and other participation in the conduct of the third-party operations. Those missions could be invited by parties to the conflict only on a voluntary basis and only with the consent of the third party'.[32] This idea was not accepted by most of the other CSCE partners, who emphasized that financial commitments could be undertaken only on a voluntary basis. Other ideas about a more institutionalized relationship between the CSCE and Russian peacekeeping forces, such as joint formulation of mission mandates or deployment of CSCE military observers to monitor Russian troops' implementation of their mandate, did not win consensus. Intensive negotiations at the December

[30] Seminar on CSCE Peacekeeping (note 29). These conclusions were later developed into a negotiating document, initially by the Swedish CIO and in 1994 by the Italian CIO.

[31] Decisions of the Rome Council Meeting, section II, para. 2, reproduced in *SIPRI Yearbook 1994* (Oxford University Press: Oxford, 1994), p. 260.

[32] From an informal Russian Federation paper, 'Further development of the capabilities of the CSCE in conflict prevention and crisis management', presented on 14 Mar. 1994 in Vienna (mimeographed).

1994 Budapest Review Conference and Summit Meeting also failed to produce a solution. The Budapest Document requested the Senior Council and Permanent Council to pursue these efforts.[33]

The basis for negotiations continued to be an informal paper under the somewhat euphemistic title 'Further Development of the CSCE in Conflict Prevention and Crisis Management', which contained the results of more than a year of negotiations.[34] In 1995 this document remained open for work, but negotiations were de facto suspended. The protracted Chechnya crisis, the absence of a Russian decision on possible OSCE involvement and a lack of enthusiasm among many of the partners removed the incentives to continue efforts. Concerns that the OSCE might be used by Russia as an instrument of its own policy were not dispelled during the negotiations.

VI. Cooperation and division of labour with other institutions

According to the 1992 Helsinki Document, OSCE peacekeeping operations are to be organized in cooperation with 'regional and transatlantic organizations'. In fact this is the only viable way of organizing effective OSCE peacekeeping. There is therefore a strong trend in the OSCE towards cooperative peacekeeping, which would reduce the burden on the UN and its over-extension in Europe.

The objective of effective OSCE cooperation with other institutions raises a number of questions. How can the overlapping of efforts and competition between organizations be avoided? How are peacekeeping duties and the use of force to be assigned to NATO, the WEU or the CIS without excluding some participating states?

The OSCE should be the first organization to initiate preventive diplomacy and peacemaking in situations involving its participating states.

NATO and the WEU may function as the instruments authorized to carry out specific tasks, while retaining their right to undertake their own actions in line with their statutes (although this would require new decisions on the future role of NATO in the European security architecture and an enhancement of its peacekeeping functions). The

---

[33] CSCE, Budapest Declaration, Budapest Decisions, chapter III [CSCE, Dec. 1994].

[34] CSCE document no. 300. In Budapest it was revised for the 10th time. It was informal and had the status of a Chairman's perception of a possible compromise.

OSCE's role should be to mandate and politically supervise the peacekeeping actions of NATO and the WEU or to subcontract to them. The OSCE can benefit from their resources and experience by requesting them, for example, to contribute to its own peacekeeping operations. Following the June 1992 Oslo ministerial decision, NATO has opened its door to such cooperation.[35] For OSCE peacekeeping missions NATO could provide logistical, transport and communications support in the form of both equipment and manpower.

Both NATO and the WEU need to develop more extensive operational links with OSCE bodies if they are to participate in OSCE peacekeeping operations. These links could be institutionalized by an exchange of letters of understanding similar to that between the Chair of the CSCE Council and the UN Secretary-General in May 1993.[36]

To make such cooperation possible in the future, extensive discussion and consultation at the conceptual level are required. An appropriate forum might be the NACC work programme for cooperation in peacekeeping. It could also be used for the exchange of experience and for promoting common training and the elaboration of common standards and procedures. Questions, however, remain: will NACC be able to develop operational capabilities? If it can, how will it interact with the OSCE? With all its weaknesses the OSCE would appear to be better equipped to fulfil operational tasks. A possible useful role for NACC could therefore be that of mobilizing political support for the goals set by the OSCE and helping to bring NATO into closer interaction with the latter.

The WEU should continue its task of strengthening its relationship with the European Union, while preserving NATO links and a US presence in Europe. This should not prevent functional cooperation with the OSCE, as exemplified by the enforcement of sanctions against Serbia and Montenegro on the Danube.

The legitimization of the actions of the CIS is problematic because it is not internationally recognized and because there is confusion over its character and structure.

[35] 'Communiqué of the Ministerial Meeting of the North Atlantic Council in Oslo, 4 June 1992', *NATO Review*, vol. 40, no. 3 (June 1992), p. 31.

[36] Framework for Co-operation and Co-ordination between the United Nations Secretariat and the Conference on Security and Co-operation in Europe, constituting an attachment to letters exchanged between UN Secretary General Boutros Boutros-Ghali and CSCE CIO Margaretha af Ugglas on 26 May 1993 (mimeographed document distributed in Vienna on 27 May 1993 by the Swedish delegation); see also UN General Assembly resolution A/48/L.19 of 12 Nov. 1993 on cooperation between the United Nations and the CSCE.

The OSCE could increase its peacekeeping effectiveness by establishing a clear division of labour with the UN. Unlike the UN, the OSCE has no mandate to conduct enforcement operations. For the time being, therefore, it must concentrate on preventive measures in the early stages of intra-state conflicts, while the UN focuses more on interstate conflicts and enforcement. This requires a further strengthening of OSCE–UN cooperation and the elimination of elements of competition, such as those that have become evident in the OSCE mission to Georgia. The agreement on cooperation of May 1993 has not yet become an effective tool and in any case does not deal specifically with peacekeeping.

OSCE cooperation with other European and transatlantic institutions awaits further exploration and appropriate political decisions.

VII. Conclusion

Three main conclusions may be drawn from the OSCE's experience.

First, the OSCE approach to conflict prevention and management and peacekeeping remains uneven. There are a number of political achievements, such as those of missions in the field; the Assistance Group in Chechnya has in particular strengthened the credibility of the OSCE. Some important tasks and challenges, as in the case of Nagorno-Karabakh, remain to be undertaken but much conceptual and administrative work has been accomplished. There is a disproportion between the verbal agreement of states to specific OSCE actions and the means put at its disposal. Other weaknesses have come to light, such as inadequate cooperation with NATO and the WEU and the lack of appropriate operational, administrative and logistic infrastructure.

However, between 1992 and 1995 the OSCE has slowly built a potential, which, although hardly noticed, may be used once the political will appears.

Second, the OSCE provides a suitable framework for seeking solutions to interstate and intra-state conflicts, being better equipped than others to deal with the former. Its comprehensive concept of security, linking human rights and political and military stability, offers a potentially unique role in preventing and solving conflicts. To date it has confined itself to politico-diplomatic or 'soft' measures of crisis prevention and management, which it is best able to use effectively and flexibly, namely early warning, fact-finding, rapporteur and monitoring missions, good offices and possibly small-scale peace-keeping operations, while leaving 'hard' measures or large-scale peacekeeping to organizations better able to undertake such military operations.[37] Criticism of the OSCE for its crisis prevention record is not always justified. It often reflects, as pointed out by Secretary General Wilhelm Höynck, the tendency of the parties to a conflict to hold the international community responsible for resolving their conflicts, in an attempt to hide their lack of readiness to compromise.[38] The CSCE's role, like that of other international organizations, is to assist parties to a conflict to solve their own problems.

Third, OSCE participation in 'hard' or large-scale peacekeeping with military involvement should not be ruled out completely. However, in such cases two conditions should be fulfilled. First, better use should be made of cooperation between relevant organizations in order both to legitimize actions taken and to ensure the provision of mutual material support. Second, the operational and decision-making capabilities of the OSCE should be further developed and strengthened, although without substantial departure from its cooperative nature based on consensus about fundamental political issues.

The future role of the OSCE in peacekeeping remains hostage to at least four political problems: protracted Western discussions on the future of NATO, Russia's inconsistent approach to the organization, the dangers of renationalization of the defence policies of the major international protagonists, and the OSCE's unpreparedness to cooperate effectively with other international organizations. However, the OSCE has great potential which may be realized if and when the major states decide to use it as an instrument to deal collectively with the challenges ahead. This condition is more difficult to meet at a time when multilateralism in the international security field is weakening.

[37] Höynck, W., 'CSCE works to develop its conflict prevention potential', *NATO Review*, no. 2 (Apr. 1994), pp. 16–22.
[38] Höynck, W., 'CSCE capabilities for contributing to conflict prevention and crisis management', Speech at the NATO Seminar in Brussels on 7 Mar. 1994 (mimeographed).

8. NATO

Steven R. Rader*

I. Introduction

For NATO peacekeeping is a new task, but it has received a great deal of attention, both practically and conceptually, since 1992. The newness of NATO's involvement in peacekeeping may seem difficult to understand given the extensive experience that many NATO members have had in UN peacekeeping, military observers having served in the earliest peacekeeping missions, UNTSO, established in 1948, and UNMOGIP, established in 1949. When UNEF I was deployed in Sinai in 1956, there were troops of NATO countries on both sides of the lines: Canada, Denmark and Norway provided contingents to the peacekeeping force, while France and the UK were belligerents.[1] The consistent pattern of support by NATO member states for UN peacekeeping has continued to the present: they provide almost 50 per cent of UNPF troops in the former Yugoslavia.

For much of its existence, however, NATO as an organization has been focused almost exclusively on Article V of the North Atlantic Treaty—collective defence against an armed attack on any member.[2] The defence of the member states has been the highest priority and will probably remain so. In recognition of the dramatic changes in Europe since 1988, NATO has begun to make significant adjustments as it prepares to meet future challenges. It is understood that the most serious risks to alliance members may come from ethnic or religious conflicts, border disputes or other problems which have the potential for regional destabilization.[3] This changed environment prompted NATO to conduct a major review of its strategy, with a resultant new direction, the Strategic Concept, approved by NATO heads of state

[1] UN, *The Blue Helmets: A Review of United Nations Peace-keeping* (UN Department of Public Information: New York, 1990), pp. 60–61.
[2] NATO, *NATO Handbook* (NATO: Brussels, 1993), p. 144.
[3] NATO, Supreme Headquarters Allied Power Europe, NATO doctrine for peace support operations, 28 Feb. 1994, p. 3 (draft).

* Sections of this paper have appeared in Rader, S. R., 'New roles for NATO: a pragmatic approach to Alliance peace operations', ed. R. Wedgwood, *Regional Organizations in Peacekeeping and Conflict Resolution* (Council on Foreign Relations: New York, 1995).

and government in November 1991. This called for a more flexible approach in which crisis management and conflict prevention would have a greater role.[4]

II. NATO's formal acknowledgement of a new mission

In response to an initiative within the (then) CSCE[5] to accept responsibility for a range of peacekeeping activities, the NATO defence ministers, meeting in May 1992, acknowledged the role NATO might play in such CSCE actions.[6] In June 1992 in Oslo the North Atlantic Council (NAC) in ministerial session reinforced that by agreeing 'to support, on a case-by-case basis . . . peacekeeping activities under the responsibility of the CSCE . . . '.[7] Subsequently NATO foreign ministers extended this commitment to possible support of UN peacekeeping missions, recognizing that NATO was ready to work with non-NATO states in the CSCE in supporting such operations.[8]

In the new security environment of Europe NATO sought to extend cooperation to its former adversaries in Central and Eastern Europe (CEE) and the newly independent republics of the former Soviet Union. The principal forum for these contacts was the North Atlantic Cooperation Council (NACC), which first met in December 1992. Although not created to be a decision-making body, NACC formed a number of cooperative working groups to develop more practical measures to bring the participants together. A particularly important component of the NACC programme was the Ad Hoc Group on Cooperation in Peacekeeping (AHG). Several subgroups of the AHG began work on common approaches to areas such as peacekeeping planning, communications, logistics, training and interoperability.[9] After their summit meeting in January 1994 the NATO heads of state and government offered a new programme, the Partnership for Peace (PFP), to draw the former communist CEE countries closer to NATO.

[4] *NATO Handbook* (note 2), pp. 153–54.
[5] The CSCE became the OSCE on 1 Jan. 1995.
[6] NATO, Defense Planning Committee and Nuclear Planning Group Ministerial Meeting, Final communiqué, Brussels, 27 May 1992, p. 2.
[7] NATO, Ministerial Meeting of the North Atlantic Council, Final communiqué, Brussels, 4 June 1992, p. 4.
[8] NATO, Ministerial Meeting of the North Atlantic Council, Final communiqué, 17 Dec. 1992, p. 2.
[9] NATO, Progress Report to Ministers by the NACC Ad Hoc Group on Cooperation in Peacekeeping, Brussels, 2 Dec. 1993, pp. 1–4.

Nations not previously identified with the Warsaw Pact, including traditionally neutral states like Austria, Finland and Sweden and new nations such as Slovenia, were also welcome to participate. In the PFP peacekeeping is clearly identified as central to cooperative efforts.[10] The separate programmes of peacekeeping activities of the AHG and the PFP were merged in late 1994 to make them complementary and not competitive.

Given the volatile conditions in many parts of CEE and the former Soviet Union, peacekeeping is very relevant to NATO's cooperation partners. In fact it is quite probable that the peacekeeping missions that NACC countries become involved in will be deployed in situations of conflict within or between NACC members. Joint work in improving peacekeeping capabilities has been intended to be seen by all, and specifically the Russian Federation, as a non-threatening form of military cooperation. These activities are not meant to be a cover for the establishment of a new defensive alliance against any nation or group of nations, despite the scepticism of certain elements in Russia.

III. Alliance strengths

The continuing tragedy in the former Yugoslavia has received close attention within the alliance. Contrary to the criticisms of its detractors, NATO has taken concrete action, in addition to lengthy deliberations among its member nations, to support UN operations. NATO officials have not sought a new mission for their organization, but rather focused on how the unique characteristics of NATO, developed over four decades, could make a contribution to international peace efforts in the former Yugoslavia.

There are several significant strengths that NATO might apply to the new challenges of peacekeeping. One of the most important is the existing multinational integrated military command and control structure. This structure was established to deal with all types of crises and has proved flexible enough to overcome obstacles in conducting successful multinational joint operations. The most recent addition to the military structure is the Allied Command Europe Rapid Reaction

---

[10] NATO, Declaration of the heads of state and government participating in the meeting of the North Atlantic Council, Brussels, 11 Jan. 1994, Press Communiqué M-1(94)3, 11 Jan. 1994, pp. 2–3; also published in *SIPRI Yearbook 1994* (Oxford University Press: Oxford, 1994), pp. 268–72.

Corps (ARRC), established in late 1992 and specifically designed to command multinational forces in a range of contingencies, including peace support operations. Virtually all NATO's military forces are national assets released to NATO for specific purposes only after agreement by both the NAC and national political authorities. Common doctrine and operational procedures and other areas of standardization have been developed over the past 40 years among the member nations and have been the key to the effectiveness of the combined NATO–WEU maritime operations in the Adriatic in support of UN-mandated sanctions against the states of the former Yugoslavia. NATO has established a solid network of infrastructure and communications systems in its member nations, especially in Western Europe, which could prove a significant advantage in mounting and supporting peace operations in or near Europe. Its air, land and maritime forces are readily deployable on short notice once the political decision is taken by the NAC. All these strengths could be used to great benefit in modern peacekeeping, especially at a time when the resources of the UN are over-committed.

IV. NATO support of the UN in the former Yugoslavia

Only one month after the NAC communiqué supporting CSCE peace-keeping activities was released,[11] the possibility of NATO supporting the peace efforts of another organization became a reality. At short notice in July 1992 NATO decided to begin monitoring compliance with UN sanctions against the republics of the former Yugoslavia, using one of its standing naval forces in coordination with a provisional WEU naval task force in the Adriatic.[12] The NATO standing naval forces have the unique advantage of being under operational command of the senior NATO military commanders in peacetime, which enables them to be employed on new missions soon after the necessary political decisions are made. As a result of the foresight of the Supreme Allied Commander Europe (SACEUR), the Standing Naval Force Mediterranean (STANAVFORMED) was positioned in the Ionian Sea just prior to the NAC meeting at which a decision on

---

[11] See note 7.
[12] NATO, Statement by the Secretary General on monitoring by NATO forces of compliance with the UN Embargo on Serbia and Montenegro, Press Release 92/64, Brussels, 15 July 1992, p. 1.

the sanctions monitoring mission was to be taken. Within hours of the political authorities making their decision, STANAVFORMED was on station in the Strait of Otranto executing its mission. In November 1992 NATO decided, in coordination with the WEU, to commence enforcing UN sanctions, in particular the embargo on trade (apart from medical and humanitarian supplies) with the Federal Republic of Yugoslavia (Serbia and Montenegro).[13] Eventually this embargo was tightened by the addition of naval patrols in Croatian and Albanian territorial waters after several merchant vessels made serious attempts to run the blockade. Finally in June 1993 the NATO and WEU naval embargo operations were given a single name, Operation Sharp Guard, and placed under a single chain of command, essentially the integrated NATO military structure, to achieve a new unity of command.[14]

The effectiveness of the maritime operation can be demonstrated by the fact that the last known attempted violations of the embargo occurred in April 1993. In November 1993 the US Government, under congressional pressure, directed that US Navy elements participating in Operation Sharp Guard should stop reporting violations of the arms embargo by the Bosnian Government and ended the provision of US intelligence relevant to violations of the embargo that might implicate the Bosnian Government. These actions, while not of overwhelming practical significance, have undermined the solidarity of NATO members and the credibility of the embargo.

The original maritime mission in July 1992 was soon followed by consultations on a possible commitment of land assets. A number of NATO nations had decided to support the UN call for forces to protect the delivery of humanitarian aid in Bosnia and Herzegovina, but only if a robust command and control structure, based on an existing NATO military headquarters, was introduced. The NAC agreed in September 1992 to the provision of staff personnel and equipment from the headquarters of NATO's Northern Army Group (NORTHAG) to form the core of the headquarters of the newly formed Bosnia-Herzegovina Command (BHC) of UNPROFOR. In the end NATO provided about one-third of the staff and virtually all of the equipment and vehicles for HQ BHC staff. Reports were very

[13] NATO, Press Release 92/97, Brussels, 20 Nov. 1992, p. 1.

[14] NATO and WEU, Joint Session of the North Atlantic Council and the Council of the Western European Union held in Brussels, Press Release 93/41, Brussels, 8 June 1993, p. 1.

positive about the impact of this arrangement in ensuring the early effectiveness of HQ BHC. Its NATO character was diminished when, because of the normal six-month rotation of UN military staff personnel, NORTHAG staff were mostly replaced by individuals from a variety of sources, only occasionally from other NATO military posts. NATO as an organization is, however, clearly able to make a significant difference during the period of great vulnerability when a new operation is being established in turbulent circumstances.

Even as the NORTHAG elements began deploying in October 1992, the UN Security Council established a no-fly zone to prevent flights by military aircraft of the warring factions over Bosnia and Herzegovina. The UN requested NATO support to monitor the airspace over the country and to assist in setting up UNPROFOR's Monitoring Command and Coordination Centre in Zagreb, Croatia. When the UN request was received, aircraft from the NATO Airborne Early Warning Force (NAEWF) had for some months been conducting training flights in the airspace of member nations and providing early-warning coverage for the maritime monitoring operations, while keeping note of activity in the former Yugoslavia. After the NAC's decision on 14 October 1992 the training flight orbits were moved to international airspace over the Adriatic in order to monitor air activity over Bosnia and Herzegovina. Two weeks later an additional orbit was established over Hungary, after a further NATO political decision and close coordination with that non-NATO country. This second orbit was essential to obtain the best possible coverage of Bosnian airspace.

The NATO air operation is an integral part of the UN mission, enabling UNPROFOR to use reports from its ground observers in conjunction with the NAEWF reports to gather the most accurate information on possible violations of the no-fly zone. In April 1993 this mission was expanded significantly to provide for enforcement of the UN restriction against unauthorized military flights over Bosnia and Herzegovina.[15] In close coordination with UNPROFOR, NATO regional air command authorities developed a smooth, professional operation that works on carefully refined and practised procedures. Apart from the period in early 1995 when the UN requested temporary cessation of enforcement activities, no request was necessary for

---

[15] NATO, NATO starts operation of no-fly zone enforcement, Press Release 93/27, Brussels, 12 Apr. 1993, p. 1.

procedures to begin once an unauthorized flight by combat aircraft on a military mission was confirmed. Appropriate warnings were given and, if there was no positive response by the violating aircraft, NATO fighter aircraft would attack.

In May 1993 the UN Security Council established safe areas around the Bosnian cities of Bihac, Sarajevo, Tuzla, Zepa, Srebrenica and Gorazde. Included in the wording of Resolution 836 was the authority for UNPROFOR to use air power to defend its forces if they were attacked while performing their duties in the safe areas.[16] This close air support capability is provided by NATO aircraft flying in combat air patrol stations over Bosnia and Herzegovina so that they are available to respond at short notice to an UNPROFOR request. Control over such close air support missions is through a network of specially trained tactical air control parties (TACPs) and forward air controllers (FACs), provided largely by the NATO countries which contribute troops to UNPROFOR. Overall coordination within Bosnia and Herzegovina is effected by an Air Operations Command Centre provided by the UK. NATO has also provided special satellite communications for the UNPROFOR TACPs to enable them to operate effectively with NATO aircraft. The air control operation on the ground in Bosnia and Herzegovina is at present entirely UN, while the aircraft and support elements for the air missions are entirely NATO.

The no-fly zone has been generally successful in preventing air-to-ground attacks in Bosnia and Herzegovina by any of the warring factions. Throughout the enforcement of the no-fly zone, however, there have been unauthorized flights by military helicopters of all three sides. The flight characteristics of the helicopters make them difficult to detect by NAEWF aircraft. Investigations of these flights by both NATO authorities and UNPROFOR assessed their activities as militarily insignificant. In February 1994 four jet combat aircraft from the Bosnian Serb side attacked Bosnian Government positions in central Bosnia and Herzegovina. The Serb aircraft were immediately warned and when they failed to respond were shot down by NATO aircraft. That was the first known violation of the no-fly zone by fixed-wing

---

[16] UN Security Council Resolution 836, 4 June 1993, p. 3. It is often overlooked that this resolution provided for air power to be used to defend UNPROFOR units in the safe areas, not to defend the safe areas themselves. This changed when the London Conference on 21 July 1995 decided that Gorazde would be protected by NATO air power. This was later extended to all remaining safe areas (Srebrenica and Zepa had by then fallen to the Bosnian Serbs).

combat aircraft since the monitoring began in October 1992. Later attacks in the Bihac area by Croatian Serb aircraft in late 1994 were answered with a coordinated NATO air strike against the runways on one of the bases in the Krajina area of Croatia used to mount the attack. When Serb attacks continued against the Bihac pocket, NATO aircraft struck Bosnian Serb anti-aircraft positions. That action produced a temporary halt in the Serb attacks, but throughout Bosnia and Herzegovina a number of UN personnel were taken hostage by Bosnian Serb forces to provide a shield against further NATO air strikes. Eventually they were released, but the hostage-taking at that time highlighted the precarious position of the UNPROFOR troops, caught between their peacekeeping mission and the enforcement actions of another organization, NATO.

The NATO authorities in August 1993 decided to prepare for air strikes in the event of warring factions continuing the strangulation of Sarajevo and other areas.[17] The targets would not necessarily be the forces directly involved in attacks on UNPROFOR forces but might be artillery positions, ammunition storage areas, command posts or similar facilities. The preparatory work paid off when on 9 February 1994, after the mortar attack on a market-place in Sarajevo, the NAC issued an ultimatum to the warring parties to withdraw their heavy weapons from a 20-km exclusion zone around Sarajevo or place them under UNPROFOR control. Violations of the ultimatum would be met with air strikes, authorization for which would be coordinated between NATO and UNPROFOR authorities.[18] The effect of this ultimatum was initially positive, in spite of periodic violations, bringing Sarajevo a significant respite from the ravages of war until fighting broke out anew in May 1995. In April 1994 the Bosnian Serb offensive against the safe area of Gorazde was first met with NATO close air support missions without major impact. Subsequently on 22 April the NAC established an exclusion zone around Gorazde and was prepared to take immediate action against violators.[19]

In May 1995 the Bosnian Serbs ended the agreed cease-fire around Sarajevo by resuming their artillery bombardment of the town. When

[17] NATO, Press statement by the Secretary General following the Special Meeting of the North Atlantic Council in Brussels on 2 Aug. 1993, Brussels, 2 Aug. 1993, p. 1.

[18] NATO, Decisions taken at the Meeting of the North Atlantic Council, Press Release 94/15, Brussels, 9 Feb. 1994, pp. 1–2.

[19] NATO, Decisions taken at the Meeting of the North Atlantic Council, Press Release 94/31, Brussels, 22 Apr. 1994, pp. 1–2.

NATO aircraft sought to enforce the Sarajevo exclusion zone by striking several Bosnian Serb targets, the Bosnian Serbs immediately responded by taking several hundred UNPROFOR soldiers hostage. Eventually the UNPROFOR troops were released, but NATO air power seemed to have lost its significance.

Concerned about the demonstrated vulnerability of UNPROFOR to Bosnian Serb military action, France, the UK and the Netherlands agreed to form and commit to Bosnia and Herzegovina a brigade-size Rapid Reaction Force, backed up by artillery and attack helicopters, to respond to any future threats. This force deployed in July and August. The Bosnian Serbs shifted their attention to the eastern safe areas, conducting a ground offensive in July, seizing Srebrenica and Zepa and threatening to take Gorazde. The NAC, meeting in emergency session in London on 21 July, warned the Bosnian Serbs that an attack on that safe area would not be tolerated by NATO. The warning was apparently heeded, since they did not attack. On 1 August NATO extended the same warning and commitment to use air power to defend the other safe areas from Bosnian Serb attack.

The Bosnian Serbs continued their artillery fire on Sarajevo until 28 August, when a mortar round killed 43 people there. NATO was galvanized into swift retaliation. Beginning on 30 August and initially for three days, NATO combat aircraft conducted over 500 missions, striking a wide range of Bosnian Serb military targets. NATO demanded that the Bosnian Serbs move all their heavy weapons outside the Sarajevo exclusion zone. On 5 September, the air strikes resumed when it was clear that the Bosnian Serbs were not taking action to meet the NATO ultimatum. In mid-September, after a 14-day NATO air campaign, which included the first use of US cruise missiles in the conflict, the Bosnian Serbs pulled their heavy weapons back from Sarajevo. At the time of writing, it appeared that recent events—the Croatian seizure of Krajina, the Croatian–Bosnian Government military successes in Bosnia and Herzegovina and the NATO-imposed cease-fire and exclusion of heavy weapons from the Sarajevo area—combined with pressure from the Serbian Government had pushed the Bosnian Serbs to the negotiating table.

Throughout the planning for and conduct of NATO air actions in the former Yugoslavia, NATO military authorities have understood that the conflict in Bosnia and Herzegovina cannot be resolved through the use of NATO air power. The ultimate resolution of the conflict will be a political settlement agreed by all parties, not imposed from outside.

During this period and continuing to the present, NATO military authorities have worked on a wide range of plans for NATO involvement in various contingencies. A high point of activity came in late 1993 with the detailed refinement of plans for possible NATO assistance in the implementation of a comprehensive peace plan in Bosnia and Herzegovina. If the parties to the conflict agreed to such an settlement, the UN Security Council might invite NATO to assume responsibility for overseeing implementation of the military aspects of the settlement and to command all UN military operations in the former Yugoslavia. The civil aspects would remain the full responsibility of the UN, although important elements of support for the civil efforts might be provided by NATO. The NATO implementation force necessary for such an operation is likely to number 50 000 troops, including the bulk of a US mechanized or armoured division, and be deployed for up to two years. In late 1994 and the first half of 1995 much of NATO's contingency planning focused on the task of forces assisting in the possible withdrawal of UNPROFOR. In the worst-case scenario that mission might call for up to 60 000 NATO troops, including 25 000 from the USA, and last six months. At present, although no details are available, NATO military authorities are apparently adjusting the plan developed to implement the Vance-Owen Peace Plan to suit the requirements for the peace settlement that the Contact Group is promoting. The size of force envisioned is very similar to that which NATO planned for throughout 1993, although the duration of the mission is now thought likely to be only one year.

The working relationship between the UN and NATO has matured and, at the practical level, cooperation and coordination between UNPROFOR and NATO's Allied Forces Southern Europe (AFSOUTH) have been close and continuous. UN–NATO relations have been built on a number of high-level contacts among the principal officials and commanders in the course of planning and conduct of these operations. There are now NATO liaison officers with the UN Department of Peace-keeping Operations in New York, at UNPROFOR headquarters in Zagreb and at HQ BHC in Sarajevo. In addition UNPROFOR has established a liaison office with the NATO Combined Air Operations Centre in Vicenza, Italy.

There have been growing pains during the development of the new NATO role of enforcer for the UN, but the results have reflected the conservative nature of NATO decision-making processes, especially when its most powerful member, the USA, is unwilling to deploy ground troops but its allies have. The consensus of the 16 member nations, each with a different perspective on the conflict in Bosnia and Herzegovina, has been to demonstrate their collective will in measured ways, cognizant of the implications for the future of Europe and for other key players, such as Russia. In several controversial decisions of the NAC individual nations supported the consensus on issues that could have had negative repercussions on their own domestic political scene. However, NATO has taken military action for the first time since its establishment and has attempted to make a difference in a turbulent situation fraught with dangers.

V. NATO's conceptual approach to peacekeeping

Progress has been dramatic on the conceptual side of peacekeeping, but the NATO political authorities have yet to agree on broad guidance as to the conditions, procedures and policies for direct or indirect NATO involvement.

At Supreme Headquarters Allied Powers Europe (SHAPE), the major NATO military headquarters for Europe, the requirement for a NATO peacekeeping doctrine was recognized and pursued beginning in October 1992. Pressure was felt from a number of nations to follow the NAC ministerial guidance and 'develop practical measures to enhance the alliance's contribution' in the peacekeeping area.[20] The areas that were suggested were logistics, training, standing operating procedures (SOPs) and communications. All these are useful areas of work, but there was one missing element: doctrine. In military operations, as in other endeavours, there must be a conceptual foundation for the practical work, a framework for logistics, training, communications, SOPs and other measures. A peacekeeping cell was formed at SHAPE in October 1992 and later expanded into an office within the formal staff establishment. In parallel with the development of doctrine, the SHAPE peacekeeping section designed, coordinated and conducted the first formal NATO course on peacekeeping at the NATO School in Oberammergau, Germany.

[20] NATO (note 8), p. 2.

The process of developing doctrine started with a review of the existing conceptual work, including various documents produced by the UN's Department of Peace-keeping Operations, the *Peacekeeper's Handbook* of the International Peace Academy, and the doctrinal work of several NATO members. Work was halted when SHAPE was directed in February 1993 to conduct preliminary planning for implementation of the Vance–Owen Peace Plan for the former Yugoslavia. This caused a delay of almost three months, but as a result the purely conceptual work that had been done was modified to reflect the practical insight gained in the course of that preliminary, but still detailed planning effort. In May 1993 SHAPE forwarded to the Military Committee (MC) its draft doctrine on peace support operations.

Work on operational aspects went partly in parallel. In late 1992, while national representatives to the NAC were agreeing on air and maritime operations in support of the UN in the former Yugoslavia, the French representative, in another forum at NATO headquarters, disagreed with the concept of NATO supporting UN peacekeeping, since the foreign ministers' statement in Oslo that June had only mentioned support of CSCE peacekeeping. Recognizing this political impasse, the North Atlantic Military Committee proceeded with the development of a document to provide high-level strategic guidance to NATO's military authorities to allow them to begin preparations for a timely and effective response to the new mission should the political authorities so direct.

This document, 'NATO Military Planning for Peace Support Operations', MC 327, was agreed by the Military Committee in August 1993. However, continuing political differences among member nations have thus far prevented the NAC from approving MC 327, leaving the alliance military structure in something of a conceptual limbo. The essential issue which has prevented progress is the competition that NATO represents to other European institutions, such as the EU and WEU, which have some claim to address security and defence matters. Leading the opposition, and occasionally its only member, has been France, which withdrew from the NATO integrated military structure almost 20 years ago. France has been consistently against NATO assuming new roles which might be appropriate, either now or in the future, for one of the other European organizations.

After MC 327 was agreed individual nations commented on the draft doctrine on peace support operations and recommended that the doctrine be revised to ensure its consistency with MC 327. Those revisions were completed and the draft resubmitted in February 1994 for final scrutiny at NATO headquarters and among the nations before adoption as an official NATO publication—if French opposition does not doom it to remain a draft for years. In July 1995 the SHAPE peacekeeping section completed a revision to the previous draft doctrine and sent it to member nations for comment.

VI. NATO's experience of the new challenges

Since 1992 NATO has had to define its conceptual position on peacekeeping while maturing significantly in terms of its contribution in the field. It has had its first out-of-area operation, its first combat mission and its first operations in coordination and cooperation with the WEU and the UN. NATO members have shown that they are ready to a certain extent to commit their common and national resources on a collective basis to support UN peace efforts. However, as a group of 16 nations operating on the basis of consensus they have their own prior expectations as to the way NATO should conduct such missions under the adverse conditions experienced by many peacekeeping missions today. The four themes that have emerged from the numerous high-level political and military consultations are political control and guidance, military command and control, tailoring the force to the mission and rules of engagement (ROEs).

Political control and guidance

NATO is an organization in which political authorities have clear primacy over the military. NATO members have shown that they accept the overarching competence of the UN, or as appropriate the OSCE, to provide the necessary political mandate for and international legitimacy of any peace operation. The NAC will carefully consider a request for assistance in the conduct of such an operation from either of these organizations, but will expect it to define its objectives clearly, including a definition of the desired end-state of the operation. If NATO accepts responsibility for the military aspects of a particular operation, it will be on the basis of partnership with the UN or OSCE in the process, not merely as a subcontractor as some have suggested.

Ultimately the solution to any conflict is political and the sponsoring organization must ensure that serious negotiations among the parties are pursued towards a comprehensive settlement. The NATO nations are unlikely to commit a substantial part of their collective or national assets to a peace operation for an indefinite period.

Military command and control

The UN has managed to operate with a degree of success in peacekeeping operations through reliance on *ad hoc* techniques and command structures. Typically in the past the force headquarters for an operation were designed by UN military staff personnel in New York who might have had some peacekeeping experience but were not responsible for executing the mission in the field. Nations then sent individual military staff personnel to an unfamiliar location to form the headquarters from the ground up. The newly arrived personnel had to learn their new responsibilities and staff procedures during the first critical weeks of the new operation. In the era of modest-sized peacekeeping forces and few challenges to their narrowly-defined authority, such an approach was generally adequate. That is clearly not the case in many contemporary missions.

NATO authorities stress the need for a robust and flexible command structure to control large and complex peace operations. It is important that the staff in control of a newly established operation are familiar with assigned duties and procedures from the beginning. This can only be accomplished using an existing headquarters structure, as in the forming of HQ BHC. The concept of a combined joint task force (CJTF) approved at the NATO summit meeting in January 1994 would provide separable but not separate headquarters and forces from within NATO for non-NATO contingency missions, a capability of significant potential for future UN or OSCE peace operations.[21]

Tailoring the force to the mission

Since the deployment of UNEF in Sinai in 1956 the tradition has been for peacekeeping forces to be primarily light infantry units equipped only with small arms. They have usually been employed in areas where two nations had reached a cease-fire agreement and occasional

[21] NATO (note 10), pp. 3–4.

violations were able to be handled without resort to the use of force by the peacekeepers. Today the conflicts which have seized the attention of the world are often intra-state, with frequent violations of cease-fire agreements. Renegade elements are not uncommon within the warring factions. Experience has shown that peacekeepers on such operations can find themselves asked to do more than originally intended. Eventually they may be called upon to implement a quite different mandate from the one for which they were organized, trained and equipped.

This volatile environment can be best handled by military forces sized, armed and ready for the threats they may face and the missions they may be called on to accomplish. NATO authorities fully acknowledge the importance of impartiality and the inherent constraints on the use of force in peacekeeping missions, but they require that peacekeepers be physically and mentally prepared for the challenges they face. This should mean that peacekeepers deploy to potentially difficult missions only with a numerically strong force equipped, like many of the contingents in BHC, with armoured vehicles and the necessary combat assets for responding appropriately with the minimum force necessary.

Rules of engagement

Traditional guidance on the use of force by peacekeepers has provided that force be used only for self-defence. However, the UN has gone beyond this restriction in several operations. Although couched in terms of self-defence, the broader rules for complex missions include using force to defend the persons and property of the peacekeeping force or persons and areas under their protection, to prevent the incursion of armed elements into designated areas, and to respond to attempts forcefully to prevent the members of the force from discharging their mandated duties.[22] These broad guidelines have provided the framework within which the NATO military authorities have developed the rules of engagement they consider appropriate for peacekeeping.

Out of the extensive contingency planning in early 1993 came a carefully developed set of ROEs that was formally noted by the NAC in July of that year. They made no mention of the former Yugoslavia

[22] Paraphrased from the ROE of a contemporary UN peacekeeping mission.

or Bosnia and Herzegovina, but provided a wide range of options for military commanders to use varying levels of force to ensure the safety of their own personnel and to enable them to perform the critical tasks envisaged in their mandate. NATO political authorities would coordinate closely with UN officials on such ROEs, including the rules that would be permitted as implementation of a peace plan began and the procedures by which further rules would be delegated to lower authorities, if and when the circumstances warranted.

Flexibility in the application of ROEs is always important in peace operations, especially as recent history has shown the volatility of local conditions and the likelihood that renegade elements may violate agreements that their political and military leaders have supported. NATO military authorities fully recognize that decisions on ROEs will be very politically sensitive and often will be taken at the highest levels in NATO and in the UN. The first priority in a peacekeeping mission will be to avoid the use of force and only then to use the minimum force necessary to resolve the immediate situation.

VII. Summary

Today and for the foreseeable future peacekeepers will be required to perform demanding missions in difficult circumstances where their lives may be at risk. NATO members have acknowledged the collective role that their alliance may play in such operations and have deployed major air and maritime assets to support the UN in the former Yugoslavia.

However, within NATO, France and the USA must reach an understanding on their roles in an alliance peacekeeping operation. The USA must provide continued leadership even in the face of domestic political opposition. The French must avoid playing the 'spoiler' to prevent meaningful NATO action in the presently unrealistic expectation that the WEU will be able to control complex military operations. Through the process of planning for and consideration of a wide range of contingency operations the NATO nations have defined their expectations of the necessary preconditions for such missions. The political will for a robust execution of the mission, including agreement on clear, attainable objectives, is paramount. From such a political commitment by member nations NATO would require high-level political authorization from the UN or OSCE, a strong, resilient command and control structure, a properly tailored and flexible force and clear guidance on the use of force. The challenges of the new peacekeeping can probably only be met with such an approach to the difficult tasks ahead.

About the contributors

Dr Hans-Georg Ehrhart (Germany) is Senior Research Fellow at the Institut für Friedensforschung und Sicherheitspolitik at the University of Hamburg and leader of its Working Group on the CIS and European Security. His most recent publications are *Crisis Management in the CIS: Whither Russia?* co-edited with Anna Kreikemeyer and Andrei Zagorski (1995), *The 'New Peacekeeping' and European Security: German and Canadian Interests and Issues*, co-edited with David G. Haglund, and 'Peacekeeping im Jugoslavien und die Folgen für die sicherheitspolitische Kooperation in Europa', *Aus Politik und Zeitgeschichte*, 6/1995.

Dr Donald C. F. Daniel (USA) is at present Milton E. Miles Professor of International Relations at and Director of the Strategic Research Department in the US Naval War College and a consultant to the United Nations Institute for Disarmament Research. His most recent publication is *Beyond Traditional Peacekeeping*, co-edited with Bradd C. Hayes (1995).

Dr Trevor Findlay (Australia) is leader of the Project on Peacekeeping and Regional Security and the Stockholm International Peace Research Institute (SIPRI). He is a former Australian diplomat and has been Senior Research Fellow and Acting Head of the Peace Research Centre at the Australian National University. His most recent publications are *Cambodia: the Legacy and Lessons of UNTAC* (1995) and 'South–East Asia' in *The International Dimensions of Internal Conflicts*, edited by Michael E. Brown (1995, forthcoming).

Angela Kane (Germany) has worked for the United Nations since 1977 and is presently Director of the Library and Publications Division in the Department of Public Information of the UN. Her previous experience in the UN has been in the Executive Office of the Secretary-General responsible at various times for political issues in the European area, human rights and disarmament, in the Office of the Secretary-General for the Central America Peace Process, and as Chief of the World Disarmament Campaign in the Department for Disarmament Affairs.

Dr Jerzy M. Nowak (Poland) is a lawyer and diplomat, presently Ambassador of Poland to the OCSE in Vienna. He is the author of

East–West Cultural Relations (in Polish, 1983) and numerous articles and studies on international relations, in particular on European security and the OSCE. His most recent publications are 'The challenges and future of conventional arms control in Europe', *Polish Quarterly of International Affairs,* autumn 1994 and 'CFE Treaty in the post-Yalta system', *Polish Quarterly of International Affairs,* spring 1994.

Steven R. Rader (USA) is Senior Policy Analyst at the Science Applications International Corporation in the USA. He was for 26 years a US Army officer, in which capacity he helped develop NATO peacekeeping doctrine and training and coordinated NATO planning for support to UNPROFOR. He recently published *Strengthening the Management of UN Peacekeeping Operations: An Agenda for Reform* (1994) and 'The US military role in an multinational framework' in *Peace Support Operations and the US Military,* edited by D. J. Quinn (1994).

Prof. Takao Takahara (Japan) is Associate Professor of International Politics and Peace Research at the Meiji-Gakuin University in Yokohama. His recent publications include 'US–Japanese military relations: towards a security community via asymmetrical integration' in *The New Europe and the World,* edited by Lawrence Ziring (1993), and 'Okinawa reversion and the Japanese "non-nuclear policies"', *International and Regional Studies,* no. 9 (1992).

Dr Dmitriy Trenin (Russia), a retired Lieutenant-Colonel of the Soviet Army, is Programme Associate at the Carnegie Endowment for International Peace and Senior Research Fellow at the Institute of Europe in the Russian Academy of Sciences. His recent publications include 'Russian peacemaking in Georgia' in *Crisis Management in the CIS: Whither Russia?* edited by Hans-Georg Ehrhart, Anna Kreikemeyer and Andrei Zagorski (1995), 'International institutions and conflict resolution in the former Soviet Union' in *European Security and International Institutions after the Cold War,* edited by Marco Carnovale (1995) and 'Non-offensive defence in the USSR and successor states' in *Non-offensive Defence in the Twentieth Century,* edited by Bjørn Møller (1994).

Index